Sridhar Seshadri is a serial entrepreneur and deep-tech expert with global experience across AI, cybersecurity and blockchain. He co-founded Spotflock, TruBitX, and Bankai Labs, building cutting-edge products in India and the US. A BITS Pilani and UT Austin alumnus, Sridhar held leadership roles at Facebook (Meta) and EA Sports, earning the CEO's Spotlight Award for Innovation at EA.

With a rare ability to simplify complex technology for business outcomes, Sridhar mentors startups at Stanford Seed, IITs, and T-Hub, helping them drive revenue, profitability, and fundraising. He also advises state government think tanks on policymaking in emerging tech, cementing his role as both a visionary technologist and an ecosystem enabler.

Shreeram Iyer is a seasoned tech entrepreneur and growth strategist, currently co-founder at TruBitX and Chief Growth Officer at Bankai Labs. He has led successful exits from AI startups and served as VP at T-Hub, shaping Telangana's startup ecosystem. Formerly Country Head – Startups at EY, Shreeram has represented India at G20 forums, advocating for startups and AI policy.

With 20+ years in global IT and strategic consulting, Shreeram holds IPs in AI/blockchain and serves on quantum and photonics committees. He advises governments via GFST and mentors startups as a general partner to family offices. An alumnus of BITS Pilani, IIM Bangalore, and CFI Canada, Shreeram blends tech expertise with policy vision and investment acumen.

For the Bold Dreamer

'This book isn't just for entrepreneurs—it's for anyone who dares to dream boldly and execute relentlessly. *The Startup Spirit* distils hard-won startup wisdom into a practical blueprint, written with the soul of those who've truly walked the path.'

—**Anil Singh**, General Manager, IIT Mandi Catalyst

For Resilience Seekers

'Startup journeys are filled with brutal setbacks. This book teaches how passion, patience and perseverance form the holy trinity of lasting entrepreneurial success.'

—**Dr Abha Rishi**, Executive Head, Madhya Pradesh Startup Center, Govt of Madhya Pradesh

'The authors have lived the start-up journey with intensity from beginning to end. Their experience plus candid approach empower them to tell the story like it is—something you will want to hear and learn from.'

—**Tariq Khan**, Partner Elevate Capital, US; Global Chair, TiE Edu SIG

'This isn't just a book; it's a blueprint for fostering innovation, revealing the raw, essential mindset that drives transformative change. For leaders seeking to ignite bold ideas and cultivate resilience, this is your compass.'

—**Ashutosh Kumar**, Senior Manager, NASSCOM

For Those Who Crave Authenticity

'Unfiltered, gritty, and deeply personal—this book isn't about glorifying success but about showing what it really takes to build something from scratch.'

—**Abhinav Gupta**,
Associate Vice President—Innovation, Broadridge

For First-Time Founders

'Reading this book is like getting a mentorship session from two battle-hardened founders. If you're launching your first venture, this is the compass you didn't know you needed.'

—**George Paul**, Head – Strategic Alliances & Partnerships, JioGenNext

For Policymakers and Ecosystem Builders

'This book offers rare insights into how governments, investors and ecosystem enablers can better support startups—from people who've worked closely across all levels.'

—**Surya Kumar**, Program Director, Ministry of Electronics and Information Technology Startup Hub

'*The Startup Spirit* is a masterclass in entrepreneurship, offering invaluable lessons on resilience, clarity and execution. Two battle-hardened founders have distilled decades of experience into this indispensable blueprint, equipping innovators and professionals alike with the mindset and strategies to navigate challenges and build impactful ventures. A must-read for anyone serious about turning dreams into reality.'

—**Sandeep Raut**,
CEO BITS Pilani, TBI, Hyderabad Campus

For Educators and Mentors

'Every startup coach, educator, or mentor should make *The Startup Spirit* required reading. It doesn't just teach mechanics—it shapes mindsets. *The Startup Spirit* is a must-have for anyone helping entrepreneurs, like coaches and mentors. It's not just a how-to guide for startups. It really focuses on building the right mindset and attitude for success. By getting into the core mindsets, the book gives coaches and mentors the tools to inspire and support new entrepreneurs. It helps them understand how important it is to be proactive, creative, and tough when dealing with the ups and downs of the startup world.'

—**Jhansi Lakshmi Gorla**,
Startup Incubation Expert, O-Hub, Odisha

'*The Startup Spirit* is a no-nonsense, practical guide for anyone looking to start and scale a successful venture. It goes beyond theory, offering real-world strategies, actionable insights, and hard-earned lessons from the trenches of entrepreneurship. From idea validation to funding, scaling, and sustaining growth, it lays out a clear roadmap to turn vision into reality. A must-read for every entrepreneur serious about making an impact.'

—**Lopa Mishra Jana**,
General Partner, Pontaq Ventures

For the Corporate Rebel

'For those stuck in the corporate hamster wheel and yearning to break out, *The Startup Spirit* offers both inspiration and a real-world map for what lies on the other side.'

—**Dr Bhanu Prakash Varla**, Serial Entrepreneur, TIE Hyderabad Board Member, Trustee IIM Bangalore Alumni Association

For Action-Oriented Learners

'Don't just read about startups—live them through the pages of this book. Real case studies, sharp advice, and founder-tested frameworks make this a must-read for doers.'

—**Arun Nagarajan**,
Partner EY, Digital Transformation

'*The Startup Spirit* isn't just a book—it's a mindset shift. Every startup coach, educator and mentor should make it required reading.'

—**Dr Raman Saxena**,
PhD Professor, SERC and Product Design
and Management, IIIT Hyderabad

'This book isn't just for entrepreneurs—it's for anyone who dares to dream boldly and execute relentlessly. *The Startup Spirit* isn't just a guide—it's Shreeram Iyer and Sridhar Seshadri's lived experience distilled into wisdom. For dreamers ready to execute, corporate rebels seeking freedom, and founders braving uncertainty, this book is the mentor they need. Authentic, practical, and deeply insightful, it lights the path from idea to impact.'

—**Rajiv Gupta**,
President, Policy Bazaar Fintech

The START UP SPIRIT

A New-Age Blueprint for Entrepreneurs

Sridhar Seshadri and
Shreeram Iyer

RUPA

Published by
Rupa Publications India Pvt. Ltd 2025
7/16, Ansari Road, Daryaganj
New Delhi 110002

Sales centres:
Bengaluru Chennai
Hyderabad Jaipur Kathmandu
Kolkata Mumbai Prayagraj

Copyright © Sridhar Seshadri and Shreeram Iyer 2025
Foreword copyright © Jagdish N. Sheth

The views and opinions expressed in this book are the
authors' own and the facts are as reported by them; these
have been verified to the extent possible, and the publishers
are not in any way liable for the same.

All rights reserved.
No part of this publication may be reproduced, transmitted,
or stored in a retrieval system, in any form or by any means,
electronic, mechanical, photocopying, recording or otherwise,
without the prior permission of the publisher.

P-ISBN: 978-93-7003-153-1
E-ISBN: 978-93-7003-860-8

First impression 2025

10 9 8 7 6 5 4 3 2 1

The moral right of the authors has been asserted.

Printed in India

This book is sold subject to the condition that it shall not,
by way of trade or otherwise, be lent, resold, hired out, or otherwise
circulated, without the publisher's prior consent, in any form of
binding or cover other than that in which it is published.

To our families

Contents

Foreword by Padma Bhushan Jagdish N. Sheth   *xiii*
Prelude: The Founder's Edge: Defiance,
Deliberation and Delivery   *xv*

1. Solving Problems That Matter   **1**
    1.1 The Entrepreneurial North Star:
        Finding Your True Problem   3
    1.2 Of Pain Points and Gaps:
        An Entrepreneur's True Compass   8
    1.3 Armours and War Chests   15
    1.4 MVP: Build, Test and Iterate   20
    1.5 The Power of Innovation in Problem-Solving   25

2. Mastering the Money Game   **34**
    2.1 Startup Economics: Understanding   37
        Financial Fundamentals
    2.2 Bootstrapping versus Raising Capital:
        What's Right for You?   42
    2.3 How to Pitch and Win Investors   46
    2.4 Managing Runway and Burn Rate   48
    2.5 Building a Revenue Model
        That Sustains Growth   52

3.	**From Zero to Hundred: Marketing and Sales Foundations**	**56**
	3.1 The Art of Persuasion and Early Sales	57
	3.2 Finding Your First 100 Customers	65
	3.3 Digital Growth: SEO, Social Media and Paid Advertisements	71
	3.4 Storytelling and Branding for Startups	79
	3.5 Building a Community around Your Product	85
4.	**People Power: Crafting Culture and Leadership**	**91**
	4.1 The DNA of a High-Performing Team	94
	4.2 Hiring Slow, Firing Fast	99
	4.3 Creating a Culture of Accountability and Innovation	104
	4.4 Managing Co-Founder and Employee Conflicts	112
	4.5 Leadership Lessons from Startup Giants	118
5.	**The Founder's Mindset: Resilience and Adaptability**	**123**
	5.1 The Realities of Startup Life: Grit and Perseverance	128
	5.2 How to Handle Failure and Rejection	133
	5.3 Knowing When to Pivot (and When to Hold Steady)	140
	5.4 Avoiding Founder Burnout and Building Mental Toughness	146
	5.5 Learning Fast and Staying Ahead of Market Trends	150
	5.6 The Enduring Impact of Entrepreneurship	157
The Entrepreneur's Leap		167
Acknowledgements		169
Endnotes		171

Foreword

In the vast universe of entrepreneurship, where dreams collide with challenges and innovation intertwines with perseverance, *The Startup Spirit: A New-Age Blueprint for Entrepreneurs* stands as a guiding constellation. Meticulously crafted for the daring souls venturing into the risk-taking world of entrepreneurship, this book offers a profound expedition into the essence of entrepreneurial triumph.

In these pages, readers will discover a treasure trove of wisdom encapsulated in twelve vital signals, each illuminating a different facet of the entrepreneurial odyssey. From the 'entrepreneurial north star' to 'passion, patience and the will to endure', these signals are not just chapters; they are beacons of knowledge, distilling the collective experience of successful entrepreneurs into actionable insights.

What sets this book apart is the fusion of theory and real-world wisdom. It seamlessly weaves together time-tested strategies and practical advice, providing a roadmap for budding entrepreneurs. Meticulously curated case studies enrich the narrative, transforming success stories into valuable lessons. These stories serve as both inspiration and a testament to the resilience of the human spirit, showcasing how determination and knowledge can overcome the toughest challenges.

The heart of this book lies in the fundamental entrepreneurial spirit—the delicate balance between passion and patience. The hidden message, 'passion and patience', encapsulates this core truth: while passion ignites the entrepreneurial flame, patience fuels its endurance. This vital lesson resonates throughout the book, reminding readers that the journey to success requires zeal and steadfastness.

As I immersed myself in the pages of this book, I was captivated by the author's profound understanding of the entrepreneurial mindset. Their ability to distil intricate concepts into digestible knowledge is unparalleled, making this book not just a guide but a mentor. It implores aspiring entrepreneurs to absorb its teachings, embrace challenges and view setbacks as stepping stones to growth.

For the ambitious minds stepping into the entrepreneurial arena, this book is more than a manual—it is a companion. Approach it with an open heart and a receptive mind. Let the signals within these pages be your North Star, guiding you through uncharted waters. May the force be with you, may you find the courage to embark on the entrepreneurial leap, armed with knowledge, passion and unwavering patience, and may your journey be illuminated by the signals of success.

—**Padma Bhushan Jagdish N. Sheth**
Emory University's Goizueta Business School

Prelude

The Founder's Edge: Defiance, Deliberation and Delivery

*'If you have a strong enough why,
you can endure anyhow.'*

—Jim Rohn, American entrepreneur and author

In the annals of every entrepreneurial journey, there exists a pivotal moment, a defining juncture that irrevocably alters the trajectory of one's destiny. For us, it occurred in the dead of night, within the confines of a small, rented office space, the kind that perpetually smelt of stale coffee and unfulfilled ambitions. The air-conditioning had long since surrendered to the oppressive heat, but neither of us noticed. Our minds were ablaze with the fervent intensity of our pursuit, fuelled by sheer adrenaline and the unwavering belief that our fledgling startup could, against all odds, survive.

We had spent countless hours, days bleeding into nights, tirelessly pitching our vision to sceptical investors, meticulously refining our product, and relentlessly iterating after each demoralizing rejection. We clung to the conviction that we were on the cusp of something momentous, something that would disrupt the status quo and leave an indelible mark on the world. Yet, in that particular moment, stripped bare of all pretence and external validation, we were simply two individuals, hunched over a computer screen, desperately trying to resolve a critical bug that threatened to derail our first major enterprise deal with a significant power generation and distribution company.

The code, as if possessed by a malevolent spirit, stubbornly refused to cooperate. Our servers, overwhelmed by the relentless onslaught of our efforts, crashed repeatedly. The clock was ticking, and we were mere hours away from a crucial investor demo that held the potential to either catapult us to success or condemn us to oblivion. Our financial resources were dwindling at an alarming rate, and the stark reality loomed large: if we failed to secure this deal, our dreams would likely crumble into dust.

I vividly recall looking at my partner, Sridhar, his face etched with an almost eerie calmness as he sipped on what can only be described as the most atrocious instant coffee ever concocted. 'We've been here before,' he muttered, his voice barely above a whisper, as if speaking more to himself than to me. 'This isn't where we lose.'

He was right. This was not our first brush with failure, our first encounter with the precipice of despair. We had both walked away from lucrative corporate careers, abandoning the allure of stability and comfort to immerse ourselves in the tumultuous world of startups. After being the first employee of Meta India and later earning the CEO award for setting up the AI and Machine Learning Department at EA Technology, Redwood City, Sridhar was heading AI as tech director at CognitiveScale, United States. I worked overseas with major clients of Tata Consultancy Services (TCS), like SAP, Deutsche Börse, Westpac, AGL Energy, etc., in Germany and Australia, in the area of IT strategy and business transformation. Both led big teams and reported to respective top management. We took our next step because the alternative—a life lived in quiet resignation, devoid of the thrill of creation and the pursuit of our vision—was far more terrifying than the prospect of failure.

That night, through a combination of sheer determination, technical prowess, and perhaps a touch of divine intervention, we not only vanquished the elusive bug but also managed to salvage the investor demo. The following day, our potential investor arrived, witnessed the culmination of our tireless efforts, and within a week, we had secured our first round of funding. We were working on an AI-based SCADA system when we were informed that positive feedback from the client would secure funding once confirmed. We needed to train our AI system to read multiple mechanical gauges, including pressure, temperature, oil levels and vibration—about 15 types in total. The computer vision device we designed in-house can work with our AI platform, but because of light issues, even with a torch, AI could not read one specific gauge because it was too old, needles were moving too fast, and numbers were not clearly visible. We tried all possible methods using standard libraries to extract numbers from images and vectors. The eureka moment came when Sridhar converted a real gauge photo into a black-and-white image, divided the dial into 360 degrees, and performed a calibration based on inputs from the factory operator over a phone call, with a few pretty bad pictures of gauges and hand drawings with approximate readings, which improved results even in low light.

It was not the funding that marked our defining moment. Nor was it the subsequent product launch or the accolades that followed. Our true triumph lay in our refusal to succumb to despair, in that act of complete defiance, and our unwavering commitment to our vision, even in the face of seemingly insurmountable obstacles. It is in that moment of completion that you, we, and anyone else who has their sights set on a bigger future realizes why those men and women who have come before us follow a singular mindset: 'It isn't over till the time you give up.' Rome wasn't built in a day, and neither was Everest scaled in a single stint. History is replete with examples of the sheer tenacity and patience that people have shown when they tried to build an organization, an idea, or an institution that was meant to last. The road, or rather trail, up to the top comes with its own pitches and forks, potholes and deviations. What separates those who make it from those who don't is first and foremost, the attitude. Unwavering determination in the face of a tsunami of foreseeable challenges and acts of god is the most basic factor in our journeys. It is when odds are against us that our true mettle is tested, and without anyone cheering, the distractions are subtracted and the audacity to succeed takes the front seat. This forms the simple formula, or rather ingredient, for every story of any startup.

Entrepreneurship, at its core, is not merely a career path; it is an audacious act of defiance. While the zeal for the term 'entrepreneurship' has come to the fore in the last two decades or so, the idea has existed even before we saw the first industries come up. In its true essential form, entrepreneurship has always meant an idea that takes shape and is put into effect to disrupt, redefine, or create a new wave. These ideas change, for the most part, the essential ways in which human society organizes itself. Contrary to the dominant narrative of entrepreneurship being a modern phenomenon, it has been at the core of our human history ever since the *Homo sapiens* multiplied. Over centuries, since the beginning of time and life on this planet, men and women have come together and organized themselves into functional units that have allowed us to form primitive communist societies. Right from the principles of barters up till the giants of capitalism, entrepreneurship has ensured that growth and development found their way forward.

The credit goes to the principles of innovation and creation because of which we now have common global economic structures, industries, supply chains and networks. The sophisticated web of global trade has become a phenomenon without which our societies and our politics would collapse—it has connected the farthest corners of the world with each other. Entrepreneurship and its tenacity have made up for what we have come to understand as the norms and rules. What differentiates the ancient ideas from the modern version of entrepreneurship is that over the years, people have succumbed to being followers. The essence of creating and nurturing leaders had taken a back seat as the world went through several ups and downs of economic changes.

For the large part, people would follow the conventional trajectory—graduate, secure a stable job, and climb the corporate ladder. The positive side of following this trajectory is that it may offer a semblance of security, but the downside is it rarely leads to the realization of one's true potential or the creation of lasting impact. True founders are not content with the world as it is; they are consumed by a burning desire to shape it, to mould it in accordance with their own unique vision.

Some founders choose to tweak the existing rules, subtly altering the parameters of the game. Others, the true revolutionaries, boldly rewrite the rules altogether, ushering in a new era of innovation and progress. It is from this spirit of defiance, this unwavering commitment to challenging the status quo that true breakthroughs emerge.

As founders who have traversed the treacherous terrain of building something from nothing, we never possessed a foolproof plan, a guaranteed roadmap to success. What we did have, however, was an insatiable drive to solve problems that others deemed insurmountable, an unwavering understanding that failure is an inevitable stepping stone on the path to greatness, and an unyielding refusal to be defined by setbacks.

We began our journey within the structured confines of corporate life, where we honed our skills, cultivated discipline, and leant the intricacies of strategy. However, we soon realized that our aspirations extended far beyond the boundaries of the corporate world. The yearning to create, to control our own destiny, and to build something of enduring value propelled us into the uncertain realm of startups. We haven't looked back ever since.

Embarking on the entrepreneurial path is arguably one of the most contrarian decisions one can make. The media, with its insatiable appetite for sensationalism, often glorifies billion-dollar exits and unicorn success stories, painting a picture of effortless triumph and overnight riches. Like every other success story that has been hounded by the media, the tip of the iceberg is glorified, and what lies underneath the surface remains hidden. Lurking in the shadows of all that shines lay the relentless battles, fraught with challenges, setbacks and moments of profound self-doubt.

The journey is paved with rejections from investors who dismiss your ideas as insignificant, months of financial insecurity as you sacrifice comfort for the pursuit of your dreams, and countless sleepless nights spent debugging code, pivoting strategies and questioning whether the sacrifices are truly worth it.

The world, in its harsh reality, does not reward dreamers; it rewards those who possess the audacity to execute, to translate their visions into tangible reality. The beauty of entrepreneurship, however, lies in its accessibility—a profound truth that democratizes the very fabric of success. It is not a gilded pathway reserved for the privileged few but a rugged, open road, beckoning to all who dare to tread it. Within this realm, the seeds of ambition, when nurtured with unwavering faith and relentless effort, blossom into fortunes that defy the limitations imposed by birth or circumstance. Understand this: the power to create, to build, to conquer the marketplace resides not in inherited wealth or societal standing but within the indomitable spirit of the individual, the burning desire to transform dreams into concrete achievements. It is a testament to the boundless potential of the human mind, a stage upon which ordinary souls, armed with nothing but their vision and their tenacity, can rise to extraordinary heights, leaving an indelible mark upon the world. Extraordinary outcomes are not the sole province of the elite; they are often achieved by ordinary individuals who possess the tenacity, the passion and the unwavering commitment to bring their dreams to fruition.

The formula for success is not luck; it is a potent combination of strategic positioning, the acquisition of relevant knowledge, and relentless execution. It is not about having the most brilliant idea; it is about possessing the grit, the determination, and the sheer willpower to make things happen. The mere whisper of an idea, however luminous, holds no dominion over the vast kingdom of achievement. It is the forging of that idea, through the white-hot furnace of unwavering grit, the unyielding hammer of resolute determination, and the relentless engine of sheer, unbridled willpower that commands the very fabric of reality to bend to one's purpose. Understand this fundamental truth: the cosmos does not bestow its treasures upon the idle dreamers but upon those who possess the indomitable spirit to seize their vision and translate it into concrete, undeniable results. It is the relentless pursuit of execution, the refusal to yield to the siren song of doubt, the burning, unquenchable fire within that transforms the seeds of potential into the towering monuments of success. For within the depths of that unwavering resolve resides the true alchemical power, the ability to transmute the raw materials of aspiration into the gleaming, tangible rewards of triumph.

THE TRIPOD OF EXECUTION

True independence extends beyond the realm of finances; it encompasses intellectual freedom, the ability to break free from the shackles of conventional thinking and embrace the inherent uncertainty of the entrepreneurial journey. But with this freedom comes a profound responsibility. Every failure, every pivot, every setback ultimately rests on your shoulders.

The most successful founders do not cower in the face of this burden; they thrive under its weight. They possess an unwavering belief in their own abilities, a deep-seated conviction that they can overcome any obstacle that stands in their path.

Consider the tale of a humble inventor, a man possessed of little more than a burning idea and an unshakeable faith in its potential. When faced with the scorn of established experts and the daunting spectre of repeated failures, he did not falter. He saw in each setback not a defeat, but a stepping stone, a lesson etched in the crucible of experience. He understood that the gold of success is not found on the surface but in the depths of persistent effort, and he pressed onwards, his resolve forged in the fires of unwavering conviction. This man, through the sheer force of his belief, transformed his vision into a reality that reshaped his industry, a testament to the power of unwavering self-belief.

The critical differentiator between those who ultimately succeed and those who falter lies in the cultivation of the age-old three essential qualities: patience, passion and perseverance.

Patience, because nothing of enduring value is built overnight. The entrepreneurial journey is a marathon, not a sprint, and it demands unwavering commitment and a willingness to endure setbacks and delays. Passion, because true founders are not merely solving problems; they are obsessed with finding solutions. They are driven by a deep-seated belief in the importance of their mission, a fire that burns brightly within them, propelling them forward even in the darkest of times.

Perseverance, because the vast majority of individuals abandon their dreams long before they have a chance to blossom. It is the unwavering refusal to quit, the relentless pursuit of one's goals that ultimately separates the victors from the vanquished.

Each of these balances the effects of others, and so one who possesses the balance of these three factors has truly unlocked the first step towards deriving the most from their life and surroundings. Without these three pillars, even the most ingenious idea is destined to wither and die.

Every successful company, every iconic brand, has faced near-death experiences and moments of profound doubt and uncertainty. The most accomplished founders do not seek to avoid failure; they refuse to be defined by it. They embrace failure as an invaluable learning opportunity, a chance to refine their strategies, pivot when necessary, and emerge stronger and more resilient.

Every setback, every misstep, is viewed as a valuable data point, a stepping stone on the path to ultimate success. This is not mere motivational fluff; it is the fundamental reality of building anything of enduring value.

We live in an era of unprecedented opportunity, where knowledge is readily accessible, funding is increasingly democratized, and technology has levelled the playing field. The true risk lies not in embarking on the entrepreneurial journey but in succumbing to fear and inaction. The cost of inaction far outweighs the potential cost of failure.

This book is not intended to be a prescriptive, step-by-step guide to launching a company. Rather, it is a blueprint for cultivating the founder's mindset, a framework for thinking critically, acting decisively, and avoiding the hidden pitfalls that prematurely extinguish the dreams of countless aspiring entrepreneurs.

If you seek certainty, if you crave the comfort of a predictable path, there are countless other books that can cater to your needs. But if you are ready to embrace the inherent chaos of the entrepreneurial journey, to take bold risks, and to build something truly extraordinary, then you are precisely where you need to be.

Let us begin.

1

Solving Problems That Matter

In the bustling heart of Old Delhi, amidst the labyrinthine alleys and timeworn buildings, a vibrant tapestry of industries thrives within modest shops. Here, one can find everything from exquisite designer *lehenga*s (bridal skirts) to weighty tomes. This vibrant, densely packed district draws thousands of employees, daily wage earners and entrepreneurs, all caught in the relentless rhythm of Delhi's metropolitan life. In this demanding environment, work often overshadows all other aspects of life, pushing health, nutrition and family into the background.

Amidst this relentless pace, those working long hours often found themselves without lunch, relying on readily available options to quell their hunger. While an unhealthy choice, it was often the only one. Then, one fine summer's day, an unassuming black-and-white van appeared on Ansari Road, filling the air with the enticing aroma of freshly cooked food. Within moments, the street buzzed with satisfied customers, their hunger appeased. For a mere thirty to fifty rupees, the hard-working men and women of Ansari Road enjoyed a nutritious meal, easing a daily anxiety. This became a pattern, and from there, what took birth was a simple business model that relied on nothing except its food, the quality of the product, punctuality and delivery. The owners, two unknown men, identified a gap in the market otherwise famous for its street food and filled it with the best possible options. They keep their menu restricted: rice with a certain number of options around the choice of lentils and vegetables, served hot and free of any unkind ingredient.

Whether this unassuming van still makes its rounds remains a mystery, but the ingenuity of its founders offers a valuable lesson for aspiring entrepreneurs. It echoes the success of countless individuals across India who deliver *dabba*s (tiffin) to officegoers in Mumbai, dinner tiffin in Delhi, Pune and Bangalore, and *thali*s (small meals) in Kolkata, operating thriving cloud kitchen businesses. Indians cherish their food, and the promise of health enhances its appeal.

The entrepreneurial spirit, whether manifested in a billion-dollar unicorn or a modest venture, thrives on finding solutions. It is the lifeblood of every dream that aspires to greatness. The most successful founders do not chase fleeting trends or build fleeting gimmicks. They identify fundamental problems, see what others overlook, and create solutions the world truly needs. If your startup vanished tomorrow, would anyone notice? If not, you are building the wrong thing. If, by any chance, this van doesn't turn up for a day, the hundreds that depend on it for their daily meals are bound to echo the complaints of going hungry. That is the everlasting impact that a venture can make. The goal, whether through a small business or a large corporation, is to become irreplaceable.

1.1 THE ENTREPRENEURIAL NORTH STAR: FINDING YOUR TRUE PROBLEM

In the vast expanse of the entrepreneurial cosmos, many a brilliant star fades before its light can truly shine. This is not due to the lack of intellectual firepower, a want of financial fuel, or even a deficiency of industrious spirit. Rather, the most common cause of their demise lies in embarking on the journey with the wrong question guiding their path.

The conventional entrepreneurial mind often fixates on 'What should I build?' This, we tell you, is akin to wandering aimlessly in a darkened room, blindly throwing darts and hoping, against all odds, to strike the bullseye. Such a haphazard approach is a recipe for failure, a path leading only to frustration and disappointment.

The true North Star for the entrepreneurial voyage, the question that separates the triumphant from the fallen, is 'What is broken?' As in the case of what we will refer to as the Mystery Van of Ansari Road, the owners recognized that the unavailability of healthy, nutritious, homemade food was the part that needed to be fixed.

A truly great enterprise does not spring forth from a mere product; it is born from a problem—a real, palpable and urgent problem that gnaws at the hearts of individuals and businesses alike. Your sacred duty as a founder is not to invent for the sake of invention but to identify and eliminate friction with the precision of a surgeon.

Consider the case of Palantir, a company that revolutionized how intelligence agencies process and utilize information. Peter Thiel, a visionary investor with a profound understanding of technological disruption, joined forces with Stephen Cohen, a brilliant software engineer, Joe Lonsdale, a strategic mind with a keen eye for market opportunity, and Alex Karp, a philosopher-turned-entrepreneur with a relentless drive to solve complex problems. These titans of technology, driven by a shared belief in the power of data to transform the world, did not merely ponder what product to build. They delved deeper, asking themselves, 'What is fundamentally broken in the realms of intelligence and security?' They saw vast amounts of information being collected but also the inability to properly use it. The answer, as revealed by his relentless inquiry, was that governments, despite possessing mountains of data, lacked the means to effectively analyse it. The true deficiency was not in information itself but in the ability to extract meaningful insights with the speed necessary for decisive action. This profound realization led to the creation of Palantir, a testament to the power of asking the right questions and relentlessly pursuing the solution.

Similarly, Zerodha, the Indian financial services giant that offers stock trading, commodity trading, and more, emerged from a similar crucible of problem-solving. Nithin Kamath, its visionary founder, did not simply see another opportunity to enter the brokerage business. He perceived an industry that was shackled by outdated technology, exorbitant costs and inefficient processes, effectively barring millions of retail investors from participating in the markets. Instead of engaging in a futile battle of features, Zerodha disrupted the status quo by abolishing brokerage fees and simplifying the investment process.

The most successful companies do not merely enter existing markets; they reshape them in their own image.

Stop Looking for Ideas, Start Looking for Inefficiencies

Alas, far too many aspiring entrepreneurs fall prey to the siren song of the 'idea trap'. They cling to the belief that their success hinges on conjuring up a brilliant, unique, world-altering idea. The stark reality, however, is that triumphant startups are rarely born this way.

Instead, they are born from keen observation, from noticing the subtle flaws and inefficiencies that plague the world around us—a truth that unlocks the very vault of opportunity. For the discerning mind, the world is a vast, untamed wilderness, teeming not with insurmountable obstacles but with hidden seams of untapped potential. It is the ability to perceive, with laser-like clarity, the friction points, the bottlenecks and the areas where progress falters that separates the visionary from the mere spectator. These perceived inefficiencies are not mere annoyances but rather the signposts pointing to untold riches, the raw material from which fortunes are forged. They are the silent whispers of the universe, revealing the unmet needs, the unfulfilled desires, and the gaps in the fabric of existence that yearn to be filled. The entrepreneur, armed with the unwavering focus of a master strategist, dissects these inefficiencies, not with the cynicism of a critic, but with a burning desire to transform them into the cornerstones of a triumphant enterprise. For in each perceived flaw lies the seed of a revolutionary solution, the potential to create a paradigm shift, and the power to command the forces of the marketplace to bend to one's will.

- Why is this process so convoluted and cumbersome?
- Why does this product demand such an exorbitant price?
- Why has no one yet stepped forward to solve this problem in a more effective manner?

The world, dear reader, does not suffer from a shortage of problems. What it lacks is individuals with the vision and courage to solve them in unconventional ways. For it is in the realm of the unconventional, where the shackles of accepted thought are shattered and the boundaries of possibility are redefined, that the true engines of innovation ignite. Conventional methods, bound by the chains of established practice, only yield predictable, incremental results. But the unconventional mind, fuelled by the burning desire to transcend the ordinary, dares to challenge the foundations of accepted wisdom, to forge new paths through the uncharted territories of the marketplace. In these uncharted territories, where the masses dare not tread, lie the most profound and transformative opportunities waiting to be seized by those who possess the audacity to think beyond the confines of the ordinary and command the forces of creation to align with their vision.

Take Airbnb, for example. It is a website and mobile app that allows people to list and book short-term rentals—an online marketplace that connects travellers with hosts who want to rent out their properties. The founders of this transformative company did not simply declare, 'Let us revolutionize the travel industry.' No, their genesis was far more humble. They were young, they were broke, and they recognized the glaring disparity between the high cost of hotels and the abundance of unused space in homes. The inefficiency was undeniable: travellers needed affordable accommodation, while homeowners had vacant rooms. Connecting these two disparate needs was the spark that ignited a multi-billion-dollar enterprise.

Had they began their journey by asking, 'What product should we build?', they might have attempted to create yet another budget hotel chain, destined for failure. Instead, they focused on what was broken and discovered a novel solution.

Every great startup is fuelled by an obsession, a relentless pursuit of rectifying something that simply cannot be ignored.

A truly powerful startup idea is not a fleeting thought; it is a persistent frustration that gnaws at your being. It is the problem that consumes your waking hours, the inefficiency you encounter at every turn, the pain point that refuses to be silenced no matter how many workarounds are attempted.

Vitalik Buterin, the visionary behind Ethereum, a public, open-source blockchain platform that allows users to store digital assets, make payments and run decentralized applications, did not embark on his quest to create another cryptocurrency. He recognized that although Bitcoin was revolutionary, it was limited in its capabilities. It lacked the functionality to create smart contracts or build decentralized applications directly on the platform. Ethereum was therefore not merely another blockchain but a paradigm shift in decentralized computing.

Similarly, Aravind Srinivas, the CEO of Perplexity AI, an internet engine that uses a comprehensive language model to process queries and synthesise responses based on web search results, did not set out to build just another search engine either. He saw that traditional search engines were plagued by intrusive advertising, SEO-driven content and irrelevant results. Instead of attempting to optimize existing search models, he forged an entirely new, AI-powered path, delivering direct, accurate answers to queries of users.

If you lack this burning obsession with a problem, you will not have the stamina to see it through to a world-class solution. The entrepreneurial journey is arduous and fraught with challenges. Without deep conviction, your motivation will falter, and your dreams will wither.

The best companies do not merely serve a market; they redefine it.

- Airbnb did not simply enhance the hotel experience; they transformed the way people think about lodging.
- Ethereum did not merely improve blockchain technology; it enabled an entirely new decentralized economy.
- Perplexity AI did not merely tweak search engines; it eliminated the need for traditional search navigation.

If your startup can enter a market and render the old ways obsolete, you have achieved a true victory. Therefore, before you write a single line of code, before you assemble your team, before you seek the favour of investors, ask yourself these critical questions:

- Is this merely a product, or is it a genuine solution to a real problem?
- Am I simply entering an existing market, or am I redefining it?
- If I succeed, will the old ways of doing things vanish into obsolescence?

If your startup were to disappear tomorrow and no one noticed its absence, then you have not solved the right problem.

1.2 OF PAIN POINTS AND GAPS: AN ENTREPRENEUR'S TRUE COMPASS

In the realm of entrepreneurship, where ambition takes flight and dreams are pursued with unwavering zeal, it is imperative to remember that the value of a product is inextricably linked to the problem it solves. Many aspiring founders, blinded by the allure of novelty, approach entrepreneurship as a contest of creativity, believing that success lies in conjuring up something entirely new. However, the truth, as revealed through the annals of business history, is that the most impactful ideas are not born from the ether but are unearthed by recognizing and addressing the real-world frustrations and inefficiencies that plague the market.

The graveyard of startups is littered with the remnants of products that were dazzling yet unnecessary, innovative yet irrelevant. In their daily lives and pursuits, people care not for mere ideas but for solutions that alleviate their burdens and enhance their existence. To build something that truly matters, one must cultivate an obsessive understanding of the problems people face, delving deep into their needs and desires.

Forget the Idea Factory: Become a Problem-Hunter

Most individuals who embark on the entrepreneurial journey begin by pondering, 'What can I build?' But the question that truly unlocks the gates of opportunity is, 'What problem is so profound, so pervasive, that it cannot be ignored?'

Consider the example of Xiaomi, the Chinese technology giant. It did not seek to challenge Apple by crafting a more technologically advanced or luxurious smartphone. Instead, it recognized critical market inefficiency: millions of consumers in emerging economies yearned for high-performance smartphones but found the premium price tags of flagship brands prohibitive. The gap between aspiration and affordability was the opportunity that Xiaomi seized. It constructed a business model that eliminated unnecessary costs, established direct-to-consumer sales channels, and focused relentlessly on delivering exceptional quality at an aggressive price. As a result, Xiaomi's growth trajectory surpassed that of its competitors, many of whom remained tethered to bloated distribution networks and outdated sales models. Xiaomi's triumph was not rooted in technological innovation but in accessibility innovation.

Spotflock, a company specializing in artificial intelligence solutions, charted a similar course. At its inception in 2017, the AI landscape was still fragmented. Academic institutions were at the forefront of AI research, while businesses and governments grappled with the complexities of integrating machine learning into real-world applications. A chasm existed between the theoretical and the practical, with groundbreaking AI models confined to research papers and academic discussions rather than being deployed to solve tangible industry challenges.

Spotflock's mission was not to become just another AI company; it was to bridge this gap by turning cutting-edge AI research into practical, scalable and user-friendly solutions across industries. The company's success was not driven by the novelty of AI itself but by its ability to address a fundamental pain point: making deep-tech solutions accessible and impactful.

Shreeram once worked with a promising startup that had developed a truly cutting-edge AI algorithm.[1] An AI algorithm is a set of mathematical instructions or rules that enable machines to learn from data, identify patterns, and make decisions or predictions without being explicitly programmed for each task.

Their technology was impressive, but they struggled to find a way to apply it to real-world problems and attract commercial interest. They were brilliant scientists, but they lacked the business acumen to translate their technological prowess into tangible value.

To help them bridge this gap, we decided to employ the problem interview method. A problem interview[2] is a customer discovery technique used to deeply understand the pain points, needs and behaviours of potential users before proposing a solution. We spent weeks interviewing potential customers across a wide range of industries, delving deep into their pain points and understanding the challenges they faced. We listened intently, not with the intention of selling our AI but with a genuine desire to understand the needs of the market.

Through these conversations, a pattern began to emerge. We discovered that the healthcare and finance sectors were particularly ripe for disruption, with numerous inefficiencies and unmet needs that could potentially be addressed with our startup's AI algorithms. Armed with this knowledge, we were able to tailor our pitch and target these industries with laser-like precision.

The results were remarkable. We secured several key partnerships with leading healthcare providers and financial institutions, leading to a series of successful pilot projects. The startup's AI was finally being used to solve real-world problems, from improving patient outcomes to streamlining financial processes. This was a testament to the power of customer discovery and the importance of aligning technological innovation with market needs.

The Pillars of Pain Point Identification

The most successful startups are founded on undeniable pain points—frustrations so deep-rooted and widespread that people are eager to pay for a solution. The challenge lies not in inventing a problem but in identifying one severe enough to demand a fix.

To guide your quest for the problem that will ignite your entrepreneurial journey, consider these four questions:

What existing solutions frustrate users?

In every industry, there are outdated systems, inefficient workflows and broken user experiences. People may tolerate these problems, but that does not mean they are content with them. The best businesses don't just create something new; they fix what is broken.

Think of companies like Ola, an Indian ride-hailing company that offers a variety of mobility services, including taxis, bikes and auto-rickshaws, and Rapido, a ride-hailing app that offers bike taxis, auto-rickshaws and taxi services in India, as well as parcel delivery and logistics services. Uber, a transport company that allows users to request rides, order food and book freight, has revolutionized the transport industry. Before these alternatives emerged, people were forced to endure unreliable taxi services, poor customer experiences and unpredictable pricing. The problem was not the transport itself but the flawed system that governed it. These startups did not invent the concept of ride-hailing; they simply removed the friction, making the experience seamless and customer-centric.

Whenever you encounter a frustrating experience as a customer, you are presented with a potential startup idea.

What inefficiencies drive customers crazy?

The most successful businesses do not necessarily create something entirely new but optimize what already exists. Amazon did not invent retail; it made buying products faster, easier and more affordable. If you can eliminate friction, simplify a process, or enhance an experience tenfold, customers will flock to your solution.

What industries still operate on outdated systems?

Entire industries are often built on legacy models that are ripe for upheaval. The longer an industry has gone without meaningful change, the greater the opportunity for innovation.

Consider the financial services sector before the advent of fintech companies. For decades, traditional banks held a monopoly on lending, investing and payments, operating on bloated fees, slow-moving bureaucracy, and rigid systems. Then came startups like Revolut, a financial technology company that offers a variety of banking services, including money transfers, travel cards and multi-currency accounts. It's available as a mobile app. Stripe, an Irish-American multinational financial services and software-as-a-service company, and Zerodha, which recognized these inefficiencies and designed solutions that prioritized the customer experience.

Ask yourself these things:

- Which industries still rely on slow, manual processes?
- Where are people forced to use workarounds because the system fails to serve them effectively?
- Which products or services seem outdated, overpriced or unnecessarily complex?
- Wherever you find inefficiencies, you will also find opportunities for innovation.
- What do people wish existed but assume is impossible?

Great startups often solve problems that people do not even realize can be fixed. They identify hidden pain points and create solutions that transform how people think about an industry.

Before Ethereum, the prevailing assumption was that

blockchain technology was only relevant for financial transactions. Vitalik Buterin, the founder of Ethereum, envisioned a broader application: using blockchain to build decentralized applications. Ethereum was not merely a cryptocurrency but a new foundation for the internet, expanding the possibilities of blockchain technology.

Airbnb's success stemmed from its founders' questioning of a deeply ingrained assumption: that travellers only desired hotels. In reality, many people had extra living space they were willing to rent out, and many travellers sought a more homely and affordable alternative to traditional accommodations. The assumption that 'hotels are the only option' was an illusion, and Airbnb shattered it.

Think about what people settle for because they believe there is no alternative. If you can provide a solution that challenges their assumptions, you have a startup worth building.

The Magnitude of Pain Determines the Value of Your Solution

The value of your startup is directly proportional to the magnitude of the pain point you solve. A minor inconvenience might generate some interest, but an urgent, costly or deeply frustrating problem will create genuine demand.

Seek out industries where customers feel trapped and tolerate inefficiencies because they believe they have no other choice. This is where the most significant opportunities lie.

The most crucial skill for a founder is not idea generation but recognizing the problem. If you can identify and articulate a problem that people desperately want solved, you are already ahead of 90 per cent of entrepreneurs.

The most successful startups do not begin with products but with problems that are too significant to ignore.

1.3 ARMOURS AND WAR CHESTS

The greatest mistake in the realm of startups lies not in the struggle for funding, nor in a tardy launch, but in the expenditure of precious time, even years, toiling away at building something devoid of market validation. The founder's vision, as compelling as it may be, must bow to the market, the ultimate arbiter. For the world cares not for your idea but for the efficacy of your solution to simplify, economize or streamline life's endeavours.

Many novice founders cling to the notion that passion alone can fuel success, but this is a fallacy. If your offering fails to elicit a fervent demand, it will merely add to the clutter in an already saturated market. Hence, validation must precede execution. Before a solitary line of code is written, a single unit manufactured, or a dollar raised, the entrepreneur must establish, beyond any doubt, that their brainchild addresses a genuine, pressing and inescapable problem.

The downfall of most startups stems not from flawed products but from products that were superfluous from the outset. Founders often fixate on developing features, refining the user interface, and raising funding, yet they stumble at the most fundamental step—neglecting to assess the magnitude of the problem they seek to solve. The remedy lies in relentless validation.

Before Airbnb's founders unveiled their platform, they grappled with a common entrepreneurial dilemma: the uncertainty of whether individuals would pay to stay in a stranger's abode. Instead of prematurely investing in technology and infrastructure, they conducted a simple experiment by creating a rudimentary website, listing their apartment and awaiting bookings. When strangers availed themselves of their accommodations, the answer was clear—the demand existed.

> Sridhar once had the pleasure of mentoring a promising startup that was developing a platform for booking home-cooked meals. The founders, a passionate pair of food enthusiasts, were eager to bring their vision to life but wisely chose to exercise restraint and validate their idea before investing heavily in development.
>
> Instead of immediately developing a complex app with all the bells and whistles, they adopted the lean startup method and created a simple landing page as their minimum viable product (MVP).[3] An MVP is the simplest version of a product that allows the team to gather the maximum amount of validated learning about customers with the least amount of effort. This landing page succinctly articulated their value proposition—connecting busy individuals with talented home cooks who could make delicious, wholesome meals—and included a call to action inviting visitors to sign up for early access.
>
> To their delight, the response was overwhelming. Within a matter of days, their landing page had attracted hundreds of sign-ups from eager customers who were clearly craving a convenient and affordable alternative to takeaway and restaurant dining. This early validation gave the founders the confidence and impetus to invest in further development, knowing that they were developing a product that addressed a genuine need in the market.

This anecdote serves as a powerful reminder that the most successful startups do not always begin with a fully developed product. They often start with a simple experiment, a low-cost way to test the waters and gauge market demand before committing significant resources. By embracing the principles of lean validation, entrepreneurs can mitigate the risk of building something no one wants and increase their chances of creating a product that truly resonates with their target audience.

Dropbox, a titan of cloud storage that allows users to store, share and synchronize files across devices, also underwent pre-validation. Drew Houston and Arash Ferdowsi, instead of immediately pouring resources into the infrastructure, crafted a video demonstrating Dropbox's functionality. At a time when synchronizing files across devices was a source of frustration, Dropbox promised a seamless solution. And the result? A deluge of sign-ups before the product even materialized, providing ample validation to commence development.

Shreeram once had the opportunity to collaborate with a dynamic startup that was developing a cutting-edge electric bike. Their passion for innovation was contagious, but they also had a keen understanding of the importance of marketing and validation. They decided to leverage the AIDA framework[4]—**a**ttention, **i**nterest, **d**esire, **a**ction—to craft a compelling video that would showcase the unique features and benefits of their e-bike. The AIDA framework is a marketing model that outlines the steps of customer engagement: capturing attention, building interest, creating desire and prompting action.

The video was a masterpiece of storytelling, capturing the viewer's attention with stunning imagery and a captivating narrative. It seamlessly transitioned into piquing the viewer's interest by highlighting the bike's innovative design, impressive performance capabilities and eco-friendliness. The video then skillfully ignited desire by showcasing the freedom, convenience and joy that owning this e-bike can bring. It finally culminated in a clear call to action, urging viewers to pre-order their own e-bike and be among the first to experience the future of personal transport.

The startup strategically shared this video across various social media platforms, targeting their ideal customer profile. The response was nothing short of phenomenal. The video went viral quickly, generating significant buzz and capturing the attention of a wide audience. As viewers watched the video, their initial curiosity turned into genuine interest and ultimately into a burning desire to own this remarkable e-bike. Pre-orders began pouring in, exceeding the startup's wildest expectations.

This surge of pre-orders not only validated the market demand for their product but also served as a powerful testament to the effectiveness of their marketing strategy. Armed with this compelling evidence of market traction, the startup approached investors with renewed confidence. Impressed by the overwhelming response from potential customers, the investors were eager to back this promising venture. The startup secured the necessary funding to begin production, and soon the innovative e-bikes hit the roads, transforming the way people commute and experience the world around them.

Great founders, therefore, test demand before committing resources. Emulate their approach by conducting problem interviews to gauge the severity of the issue you want to solve. Engage in direct conversations with potential users, probing their current solutions, workarounds and past expenditures on similar products. If the problem isn't a burning pain point, your startup will struggle to gain traction.

The most potent indicator of demand is pre-sales. If customers are unwilling to place a pre-order, join a waitlist, or pay a deposit, they are unlikely to convert into paying customers. This strategy has been employed by industry giants such as Tesla, which takes pre-orders before manufacturing new models, and Superhuman, the premium email app that built a waitlist of thousands before launch.

Another effective validation technique is the fake-it-till-you-make-it approach, simulating the solution with minimal effort. For example, Zappos, an online retailer that sells shoes, clothing, handbags and accessories, initially fulfilled orders manually from local stores after customers placed orders on its website. This strategy mitigates the most significant risk for startups—building something unwanted.

Every hour invested in validation can save weeks of wasted effort. The right launch strategy isn't to build first and hope, but to rigorously test, refine and validate until you are certain your startup addresses a problem that people are willing to pay to solve. Find the pain point, talk to users, secure early commitments, and simulate the product if necessary. An idea remains invalidated until the market deems it worthy. If no one expresses interest, move on and find a problem that truly resonates with potential customers.

1.4 MVP: BUILD, TEST AND ITERATE

The minimum viable product (MVP) is not about achieving perfection on its initial launch but rather a strategic endeavour to test the fundamental concept with the least amount of exertion. It is precisely at this juncture that a multitude of founders falter, succumbing to the pitfalls of either excessive or insufficient development. Overbuilding entails dedicating months, even years, to crafting superfluous features that remain unsolicited by the intended audience. Conversely, underbuilding manifests itself in the release of a product that is so rudimentary that it fails to showcase any genuine value proposition. Both avenues ultimately lead to failure. Overbuilding leads to the squandering of precious resources, while underbuilding culminates in a lack of adoption. The most effective MVPs are not necessarily feature-rich; instead, they are problem-rich. They address a single, critical frustration with such efficacy that users can no longer disregard them.

Contrary to popular belief, founders do not require a fully functional product to get their company off the ground. What they truly need is irrefutable proof that the market wants the solution they are offering. Your MVP should focus on one fundamental question: Do people care enough about this problem to pay for a solution? The most effective way to validate this is to reduce your product to its core value. If your MVP cannot prove that people really want what you're offering, no number of additional features will save it.

Jeff Bezos founded Amazon, a multinational online retailer that sells a variety of products and offers cloud computing, digital streaming and artificial intelligence (AI), not with the grand vision of a global retail empire. Such an undertaking would have been too ambitious, complex and costly. Instead, he posed a simple question: What is the most straightforward way to prove the efficacy of e-commerce? His answer? A bookshop. Books were easily categorized, had consistent pricing, and did not require customers to try them before purchasing. Selling books online proved the viability of e-commerce, and only after validating demand did Amazon expand into other categories.

> Picture this: a fledgling online grocery delivery startup, brimming with ambition but facing the daunting task of entering a crowded market. They had a vision—to revolutionize the way people buy groceries—but they were wise enough to know that a grand entrance with a full-fledged app and a vast inventory could be a recipe for disaster.
>
> That's where I came in. I advised them to adopt a 'pilot market strategy',[5] a controlled rollout that would allow them to test the waters before diving head first into the deep end. A pilot market strategy is a low-risk approach where a product or service is launched in a limited geographic or demographic segment to test viability before rolling it out on large scale. Instead of overinvesting in a complex app, a simple, user-friendly website was launched with a limited selection of products, focused on a specific geographical area.
>
> This approach proved to be a game changer. By limiting the initial scope, they were able to validate demand, fine-tune their delivery operations, and gather valuable customer feedback without the risk of overspending or spreading themselves too thin. They learnt what worked and what didn't, and most importantly, what their customers truly wanted.

> The pilot market became their testing ground, a microcosm of the larger market, where they could experiment, adapt and optimize before scaling up their operations. It was a classic example of 'think big, start small, scale fast'.

Similarly, Lei Jun did not launch Xiaomi, a Chinese company that manufactures smartphones, smart home devices and other consumer electronics, with a complete hardware lineup. He did not need to either. Instead of spreading resources thin, Xiaomi released a high-quality smartphone at an unbeatable price. Xiaomi built a loyal customer base by perfecting a single product and focusing on price-to-performance value before expanding into other product categories such as wearables, smart televisions and home automation.

> Sridhar once had the pleasure of mentoring a dynamic startup that was venturing into the exciting world of smart home devices. They were brimming with innovative ideas for an entire ecosystem of interconnected gadgets but wisely chose not to spread themselves too thin at the outset.
>
> Instead, they strategically applied what he likes to call the 'bowling pin strategy'.[6] They identified their 'head pin'—a smart speaker that would serve as their initial beachhead product. The bowling pin strategy is a go-to market approach where a company first targets a specific, high-impact market segment (head pin) and then gradually expands into adjacent segments, to build momentum, like knocking down pins on a bowling alley.
>
> This was a strategic move, as a smart speaker could be easily adopted by consumers and would serve as a

> central hub for the future ecosystem. They initially focused on perfecting this head pin to ensure that it delivered a delightful user experience and garnered rave reviews.
>
> Once the smart speaker gained traction and established its credibility in the market, the company began to systematically 'knock down' adjacent pins. They leveraged their growing customer base and brand recognition to expand into complementary product categories, such as smart lighting and security systems. This measured, strategic approach allowed the company to grow sustainably, solidifying its position in the market with each successful product launch.
>
> Simultaneously, he guided them through the principles of the lean startup methodology, emphasising the importance of building an MVP as quickly as possible. This meant focusing on the core features that brought the most value to customers and iterating rapidly based on user feedback. By combining the bowling pin strategy with the lean startup approach, this promising startup managed to navigate the treacherous waters of entrepreneurship with remarkable agility and efficiency.

Building an MVP isn't about launching a half-baked product but about proving that your core solution is valuable. Here's how you do it: Every MVP should be built around a primary pain point. Ask yourself: What is the No. 1 problem I'm solving? Can I eliminate all other distractions and still provide value? Would users still pay for it if I removed everything except the core solution? If your MVP tries to do too many things, it's not an MVP—it's a half-finished product. The simpler the solution, the easier it is to validate. A common mistake first-time founders make is to wait until everything is 'perfect' before launching. Nothing is ever perfect. If you wait too long, you'll waste months (or years) working on something that may not even be relevant at the time of launch. Consider Perplexity AI, an AI-powered search engine that uses natural language processing to answer questions. It's designed to provide accurate, relevant answers in real time and is a great example. Instead of spending years developing a fully optimized AI-driven search engine, Perplexity started with a basic AI-powered Q&A system to validate demand before scaling up. By launching early, they received real-world feedback that helped them refine the product instead of relying on assumptions. If you are not embarrassed by your first version, you have started too late.

The biggest mistake you can make is to test your MVP with people who don't represent your actual customers. Friends, family and colleagues will tell you what you want to hear, but real users will tell you what you need to hear. Your MVP is a success when people use it without being forced to. Early users recommend it to others. Someone is willing to pay for it. If none of these things happen, your product can't solve a big enough problem. Once your MVP is live, track the metrics that indicate whether your idea is worth pursuing. Ignore vanity metrics like website traffic and focus on accurate validation indicators:

- **Engagement**: Are people using your product repeatedly?
- **Retention**: Do users come back after the first experience?
- **Conversion**: Are people willing to pay for what you've built? It's time to iterate or pivot the product if the data shows weak traction.

The purpose of an MVP isn't to prove that your idea is perfect—it's to find out where it's wrong so you can improve it quickly. Before founding Ethereum, Vitalik Buterin recognized that blockchain technology had limitations—Bitcoin was too rigid to support decentralized applications. Instead of theorizing endlessly, he created a whitepaper, gathered feedback and adjusted his approach. Only after significant iterations did Ethereum evolve into a full-fledged platform.

Your first version will have flaws—that's inevitable. What matters is how quickly you recognize them and adapt. Your MVP is not the final product—it's an experiment designed to validate (or disprove) your assumptions. This is the reality: If no one wants your MVP, no amount of marketing can save it. Your business model is weak if people use it but don't pay for it. If users love it and actively recommend it, you've found something worth scaling. A great MVP lets the market decide what comes next. If users embrace it, refine, improve and expand it. If users ignore it, pivot or move on. The worst thing a founder can do is fall in love with their idea instead of what the market needs. The goal is not to build the product you want, but the product that customers can't live without. Your MVP exists to test reality. If users adopt it, engage with it, and demand more, you've found a way forward. If not, it's time to rethink your approach. Before you invest heavily in development, scaling or fundraising, ensure your MVP has passed the only test that matters: Does the market want it?

1.5 THE POWER OF INNOVATION IN PROBLEM-SOLVING

At its core, innovation is about finding solutions to problems and not merely inventing novelties. Many believe that innovation is synonymous with groundbreaking inventions, yet this is a misconception. The most successful companies don't begin by creating something entirely new; they start by addressing existing issues and improving what already exists.

True innovation isn't about waiting for a sudden flash of inspiration. It's a process that involves iteration, pattern recognition and relentless execution. The most accomplished founders don't stumble upon brilliant ideas overnight; they observe inefficiencies, eliminate friction, and tackle problems that others overlook.

Consider Airbnb, for instance. It wasn't the first platform to offer short-term accommodations, but it was the first to empower homeowners to monetize their unused space on a large scale. Instead of competing directly with hotels, Airbnb revolutionized consumer behaviour by making peer-to-peer lodging mainstream.

> Shreeram once had the opportunity to collaborate with a dynamic startup that was revolutionizing the commercial real estate landscape. Their innovative platform addressed a common problem faced by businesses of all sizes—underutilized office space. By leveraging the power of the platform business model,[7] they created a vibrant marketplace where businesses with excess space could connect with those in need of flexible, cost-effective workspace solutions.
>
> The platform business model is a value-creation strategy where a company facilitates exchanges between two or more interdependent user groups—typically consumers and producers—through a digital infrastructure that benefits from network effects.

The beauty of their approach lay in their understanding of network effects. The more businesses listed their available spaces on the platform, the more attractive it became for potential renters. Conversely, as the number of renters increased, more businesses were incentivized to join the platform, creating a virtuous cycle of growth and value creation.

Their success wasn't solely attributable to network effects. They also invested heavily in optimizing their matching algorithms, ensuring that businesses and renters were connected seamlessly based on their specific needs and preferences. Furthermore, they recognized the importance of liquidity in the marketplace. Focusing on creating a critical mass of supply and demand ensured that transactions could be completed quickly and efficiently, further fuelling the platform's growth.

Through its innovative approach and relentless execution, this startup not only created a thriving new market but has also challenged the traditional, often inefficient, real estate sector. They demonstrated the power of platform thinking and the transformative potential of technology to address real-world problems and create value for all stakeholders.

Perplexity AI didn't invent the search engine. However, it recognized a growing user need for direct, conversational answers instead of sifting through endless links. By leveraging AI-powered retrieval models, Perplexity created a more intuitive, user-focused way to find information and eliminate the inefficiencies of traditional search engines.

In the ever-evolving landscape of technological innovation, Sridhar had the privilege of advising a fledgling startup that dared to challenge the established giants of the search engine realm. This intrepid team, driven by a shared passion for user-centred design and a deep understanding of the frustrations that plagued users of conventional search engines, embarked on a mission to redefine the search experience.

They recognized that the search landscape was dominated by behemoths that prioritized complex algorithms and an overwhelming wealth of information, often at the expense of simplicity and user-friendliness. However, the founders of this startup envisioned a search engine that would serve as an intuitive extension of the user's mind, a tool that would seamlessly anticipate their needs and deliver precisely the information they sought with minimal effort.

To achieve this ambitious goal, they embarked on a meticulous process of user research,[8] engaging in countless hours of interviews and feedback sessions with individuals from all walks of life.

User research is the process of systematically studying target users through methods such as interviews and observation to understand their behaviours, needs and pain points in order to design better, user-centered products.

They sought to understand the nuances of how people interact with search engines, the pain points they encounter, and the desires that remain unfulfilled.

Armed with this invaluable knowledge, the team set about crafting a search engine that prioritized clarity, simplicity and an unwavering focus on the user experience.

> They stripped away the unnecessary clutter and distractions that characterized traditional search engines, replacing these with a clean, minimalist interface that prioritized the presentation of relevant information in a concise and easily digestible format.
>
> They also leveraged cutting-edge natural language processing technology to enable users to interact with the search engine in a more conversational manner, as if they were talking to a knowledgeable friend. This approach not only simplified the search process but also fostered a sense of connection and trust between the user and the search engine.
>
> Through their relentless pursuit of user-centred design and unwavering commitment to simplifying the search process, this startup was able to carve out a unique niche in a fiercely competitive market. They attracted a loyal following of users who appreciated the elegance, efficiency and intuitiveness of their search engine, and they quickly gained recognition as a formidable force in the world of search.
>
> The success of this startup serves as a testament to the power of user-centred design and the importance of addressing genuine pain points in the marketplace. By focusing on the needs of their users and relentlessly pursuing simplicity and ease of use, they were able to differentiate themselves from the competition and build a product that truly resonated with their target audience.

Similarly, Vitalik Buterin's Ethereum wasn't the first cryptocurrency, but it addressed Bitcoin's most significant limitation. Bitcoin—the first decentralized cryptocurrency—is based on a free-market ideology and was invented in 2008 by Satoshi Nakamoto (an unknown entity). Ethereum introduced smart contracts, enabling decentralized applications and redefining the potential of blockchain technology. It wasn't just a new product—it became the foundation for an entire industry.

This is what real innovation looks like—not a sudden stroke of genius, but an unwavering dedication to solving problems better than anyone else.

How to Innovate in a Meaningful Way

If your goal is to build a lasting business, don't start by asking yourself, 'What product should I build?' Ask instead:

- What is broken?
- What causes people the most frustration?
- Which industry is stuck in outdated models?
- How can I remove unnecessary friction from a process?

The future belongs to those who solve the biggest problems in the simplest ways.

Consider how the most innovative startups have transformed their industries:

- Uber obliterated the frustration of hailing taxis by cutting down waiting times and simplifying payments.
- Tesla, an American company that designs, manufactures and sells electric vehicles, solar panels and energy storage systems, didn't invent electric cars—it made them desirable and mainstream through innovating in battery efficiency, software and branding.

- Stripe didn't invent online payments but simplified them. While banks made payment processing complex, Stripe turned it into a few lines of code.

The common thread is that they didn't invent new industries—they removed barriers, simplified processes, and created experiences that customers couldn't ignore.

Build Something That Would Be Missed if It Disappeared

A simple test of whether your startup is solving a real problem is to ask yourself: If your company disappeared tomorrow, would anyone care?

- Would customers scramble to find an alternative?
- Would the industry sense a gap that needs to be filled?
- Would people be frustrated that your solution is no longer available?

If the answer is no, your startup is not solving a fundamental problem. Lasting companies are not built on hype but on necessity.

The most successful startups aren't just exciting—they're indispensable.

- Google, an American company that provides internet services, including search, cloud computing and software, isn't just a search engine; it's the way we navigate the internet.
- WhatsApp, a free messaging app that allows users to send and receive texts, photos, videos and more, isn't just a messaging app; it's the way billions of people around the world communicate.

If your product vanishes and your users simply move on, your startup isn't solving a problem deeply enough. Make your product so indispensable that the world can't function without it.

Execution over Ideas: Make Innovation Happen

Innovation doesn't happen when you just think about ideas—it comes from execution.

If you want to innovate in a way that matters:

- Find what's broken. Don't just brainstorm new products; identify inefficiencies.
- Make something exclusive and accessible. The best businesses democratize access—for example, Robinhood, a financial services company that allows users to buy and sell stocks, exchange-traded funds (ETFs), cryptocurrencies and options, and Coursera, an online learning platform that offers courses, degrees and certificates from universities and companies.
- Eliminate unnecessary complexity. If something is too complicated, simplify it, such as Zoom, a cloud-based video conferencing platform that allows users to communicate with each other via audio and video, and Canva, an online design platform that allows users to create a variety of visual content.
- Create frictionless experiences. Remove unnecessary steps, reduce waiting times, and optimize usability.

Startups that fundamentally change industries don't just create new things—they also make the old way of doing things obsolete.

Innovation Is a Process, Not a One-Time Event

Most founders think innovation means a big breakthrough. In reality, however, innovation is a continuous process of testing, refining and improving.

- Amazon started as an online bookshop and expanded into e-commerce, cloud computing and AI.
- Airbnb began with spare-room rentals but became an alternative to hotels, business travel and even luxury stays.

Your first version won't be perfect. Nor is it meant to be. The only question that matters is: Are you making progress every day?

The World Needs More Problem Solvers, Not More Startups

We don't need more startups. We need more solutions.

The best entrepreneurs don't just launch businesses; they fix inefficiencies, rethink industries, and challenge the status quo.

If you want to build something that lasts, forget chasing 'startup ideas'. Look for real problems that need to be solved.

- The best ideas don't come from imagination. They come from insight.
- If you truly solve a problem, success is inevitable.
- Great founders don't just build companies—they build things that matter.

If you're ready to stop chasing trends and start solving real problems, you're on the right path.

2

Mastering the Money Game

Money represents a curious paradox in the realm of startups. It is the lifeblood that sustains the company, and yet the relentless pursuit of it can lead to ruin. Many a founder has been undone not because of a lack of funds but by a failure to grasp the art of management. A successful startup not merely acquires capital but also understands the precise timing, the underlying purpose, and the prudent methods for deploying it. The money game transcends the mere act of raising funds; it lies in the wisdom of its use. If the burn rate remains unchecked, if financial decisions lack sagacity, and if a sustainable revenue model proves elusive, then the startup's existence is precarious, and its days are numbered.

Fundraising coupled with financial discipline dictates the lifespan of a nascent enterprise. Cash flow reigns supreme. The annals of entrepreneurship abound with tales of founders whose visions birthed groundbreaking products, but those same visionaries often met their downfall, their ambitions dashed on the rocks of financial ignorance. Running a startup is not solely about aligning the product with the market; it is a testament to financial acumen. The entrepreneur is not merely building a company but is entrusted with the stewardship of capital in an environment that seems designed for their destruction.

Why Startups Run out of Money

The crux of the matter lies in the negative cash flow. Unlike established businesses, which generate revenue from their inception, startups typically have to endure a period of cash burn before profitability emerges. This is tenable only if a financial blueprint exists, one that provides sufficient runway to reach profitability or secure the next round of funding. Yet, many founders stumble over the same three pitfalls.

Premature scaling

The allure of expansion can be intoxicating, leading to the premature hiring of a large team, extravagant marketing expenditures before demand is proven, and ventures into new markets before dominance in existing ones is established. These are classic blunders that drain resources at an alarming speed.

Housing.com, a real estate portal that helps users find properties to rent or buy in India, serves as a cautionary tale. Once a promising real estate startup, the portal amassed millions in funding but succumbed to the siren song of rapid scaling. Operations expanded, employees were hired en masse, and branding expenses spiralled out of control. The consequences were dire. The company depleted its funding before achieving sustainable revenue, forcing leadership changes and ultimately forfeiting its market advantage. The lesson is clear: growth is desirable, but only if it is sustainable.

Ignoring unit economics

Startups often fixate on top-line growth, captivated by metrics such as revenue and user acquisition. However, the true measure lies in unit economics—the profitability of the business model on a per-customer basis. Selling a product at a loss and clinging to the hope that profitability will magically mend the latter is a perilous gamble.

Grofers (now Blinkit), an online grocery shopping app that delivers groceries and other items to customers in India, exemplifies this pitfall. Initially, Grofers embraced a deep discounting model to lure customers, operating with negative margins under the assumption that the costs would be recouped as they scaled. Instead, losses mounted, compelling the company to pivot into instant grocery delivery. Today, Blinkit survives under the Zomato umbrella, but the lesson remains: blind growth without profitable unit economics is unsustainable.

Miscalculating runway

Runway, the critical measure of how long a startup can survive at its current burn rate, can be a fatal miscalculation. If cash reserves dwindle before the next milestone is reached, the enterprise falters.

Argo AI, a company that developed self-driving technology for vehicles in the US, and an autonomous vehicle startup, enjoyed the backing of Ford and Volkswagen, raising over $2.6 billion. However, in 2022, both companies withdrew their funding, citing Argo AI's lack of a transparent revenue model. The company spent profligately without a clear path to profitability. The result was swift and brutal: Argo AI was shut down overnight.

The message is stark: Without control over the runway, a startup cannot endure long enough to achieve success.

2.1 STARTUP ECONOMICS: UNDERSTANDING FINANCIAL FUNDAMENTALS

To succeed in the grand game of business, one must possess an unwavering grasp of its financial intricacies. A founder oblivious to their startup's financial health is akin to a ship's captain navigating treacherous waters without a compass. Let us delve into the key figures that illuminate the path to prosperity.

The Numbers That Matter

1. **Burn rate:** This metric reveals the rate at which your financial resources are consumed each month. A high burn rate, unaccompanied by sufficient revenue, signals a perilous situation, much like a furnace burning through fuel without producing adequate heat. The formula is straightforward:

    Total monthly expenses = Burn rate

2. **Runway:** This critical measure indicates the time remaining before your financial reserves are exhausted. Should your runway dwindle to less than 12 months, it is a clarion call for decisive action. Curtailing expenses or securing additional funding becomes imperative. The calculation is simple:

    Runway = Total cash / Burn rate

3. **Customer acquisition cost (CAC):** This figure represents the expenditure incurred to acquire a single paying customer.

Too high a CAC renders your business model unsustainable, like a farmer sowing seeds that yield no harvest. The formula is:

$$CAC = \text{Total sales and marketing spend} / \text{New customers acquired}$$

CRED, a members-only app that helps users manage their finances, pay bills and earn rewards, serves as a prime example. Their aggressive marketing strategy aimed at attracting high-value credit card users came at a significant cost. The gamble was that a valuable user base could be built, but the risk was clear: failure to monetize this base would render the venture unsustainable.

> Sridhar once had the opportunity to mentor a promising startup that was struggling to achieve sustainable growth despite its innovative product and aggressive marketing efforts. The company was burning through its seed funding at an alarming rate, but customer acquisition costs remained stubbornly high and profitability was elusive.
>
> It was clear that something was amiss. We decided to take a deep dive into their unit economics,[9] dissecting their customer acquisition funnel and analysing the lifetime value of their customers. What we discovered was a classic case of misallocated resources. The company was invested heavily in marketing channels that were generating leads but not attracting the kind of customers who would not only buy their product but also remain loyal over the long term.
>
> Unit economics refers to the direct revenues and costs associated with a single unit of a product or service, helping businesses assess profitability on a per-customer or per-transaction basis.

> We worked closely with the founders to reallocate their marketing budget and shift focus to higher ROI channels that were more likely to attract high-value customers. We also helped them refine their pricing strategy and optimize their customer onboarding process to improve customer retention.
>
> The results were remarkable. Within a few months, customer acquisition costs dropped significantly, customer lifetime value increased, and the company's profitability soared. They had successfully transformed their business from a cash-burning machine into a sustainable, thriving enterprise.
>
> This experience reinforced for me a fundamental principle of entrepreneurship: It's not just about acquiring customers, it's about acquiring loyalty.

4. **Customer lifetime value (LTV):** This metric represents the total revenue generated by a customer throughout their association with your business. A prudent rule of thumb dictates that LTV should be at least three times your CAC. The formula is:

$$LTV = \text{Average revenue per user (ARPU)} \times \text{Customer lifetime}$$

Razorpay, a fintech startup, prioritized a healthy LTV to CAC ratio from its inception. Focusing on businesses with high customer retention instead of unsustainable customer acquisition fostered robust unit economics and paved the way for profitable scaling.

> Sridhar once worked with a startup that was laser-focused on acquiring as many customers as possible. Their mantra was 'growth at all costs', and they poured all their resources into marketing and sales, aiming to dominate the market share. While customer volume increased significantly, profitability stagnated. They were trapped in a cycle of acquiring customers who weren't contributing to their bottom line.
>
> It became clear that they needed a shift in strategy. We implemented customer segmentation and LTV analysis to better understand the customer base. This revealed a surprising insight: a small segment of high-retention and high-value customers was generating a disproportionate amount of revenue. These customers were not only loyal but also very profitable in the long run.
>
> Armed with this knowledge, the startup refocused its marketing and sales efforts on attracting and retaining these high-value customers. They tailored their messaging, personalized their offerings, and built stronger relationships with this segment. The result was a significant improvement in unit economics and a more sustainable growth trajectory.

5. **Gross margins:** This percentage reveals the revenue remaining after deducting the cost of goods sold (COGS). Software startups typically enjoy gross margins of over 80 per cent, while physical product startups operate in the 20–40 per cent range. Slender margins impede scaling efforts—much like a bird with clipped wings struggles to soar. The formula is:

Gross margin = (Revenue - COGS) / Revenue × 100

Tesla disrupted the automotive industry not only with its innovative EV technology but also by expanding its gross margins. By adopting a direct-to-consumer sales model, Tesla bypassed traditional dealerships, increasing its margins and gaining a competitive advantage over legacy automakers burdened by outdated cost structures.

Cash Flow Management Is Survival

In the realm of startups, money is not merely fuel; it is the oxygen that sustains life. A brilliant idea starved of financial nourishment will wither and perish before it can bear fruit. To master your financial destiny, adhere to these principles:

- **Meticulous tracking:** Maintain a vigilant eye on every rupee, every dollar. Your financial numbers should never catch you off guard.
- **Ruthless efficiency:** Be relentless in scrutinizing your expenses. If expenditure does not contribute to revenue generation or survival, it must be eliminated.
- **Judicious fundraising:** Seek only the capital that is truly necessary. An overabundance of funds can be just as detrimental as scarcity.
- **Revenue priority:** Before embarking on a quest for user acquisition, ensure that you are building something that people are willing to pay for.

The Two Clocks of a Startup

Every startup operates under the tyranny of two clocks:

1. **The vision clock:** It measures the speed at which you can develop your product and gain traction in the market.

2. **The financial clock**: It dictates how long your financial resources can sustain your venture.

Should the financial clock strike midnight before the vision clock reaches its goal, your startup's journey will come to an abrupt end. The most astute founders prioritize mastery of startup economics over the pursuit of investors, growth or fleeting headlines. For in the end, cash flow reigns supreme, and the one who commands it most effectively emerges triumphant.

2.2 BOOTSTRAPPING VERSUS RAISING CAPITAL: WHAT'S RIGHT FOR YOU?

Every entrepreneur faces a fundamental question: Should you bootstrap your business or should you seek funding from venture capitalists? The answer is not a matter of ideology but a matter of strategy. It depends entirely on the nature of your business, the speed at which you need to grow, and the trade-offs you are willing to make.

Some of the most successful businesses in the world were built without raising a single dollar from investors. Others would not exist without massive capital injections. The key is to understand what your startup needs, not what the ecosystem expects.

The Power of Bootstrapping

Bootstrapping allows a business to be profitable from day one. Some of the best companies—Zoho (India), a collection of cloud-based business applications that help with productivity, collaboration and more; Mailchimp (USA), a marketing platform that helps businesses manage and grow their customer base; Basecamp (USA), a web-based project management tool that helps teams organize work, share updates and track progress; and Spanx (USA), a shapewear brand that includes bodysuits, underwear and other innerwear and outerwear—were bootstrapped. They remained lean, focused and independent. Instead of chasing VC money, they built sustainable businesses that paid for themselves.

Bootstrapping is not about rejecting VC funding; it's about proving that your business can generate revenue independently. If you can sustain and grow without external funding, you retain full control and are not tied to investors with aggressive timelines.

Bootstrapping is the right path if: Firstly, your business can generate revenue early on. If you sell a product or service with upfront payments or short sales cycles, you can reinvest the profits into growth. Secondly, you have personal savings or a way to sustain yourself. Bootstrapping doesn't mean you don't need capital—it means the capital comes from your own savings, revenue or alternative sources such as grants and loans. Lastly, you don't want external pressure from investors. The moment you accept VC funding, the clock starts ticking for you. Investors expect growth, milestones and a return on investment. Bootstrapped companies can control their own pace and make long-term decisions without investor interference.

The Case for Raising Capital: Speed and Scale

Some industries demand capital to be competitive. If you're building something that requires mass adoption, physical infrastructure, or heavy research and development, bootstrapping isn't an option—you need external funding.

Raising VC money isn't inherently good or bad—it's a tool. The best founders know why they are raising money, how much they need, and what milestones they will reach.

VC funding is the right choice if: Firstly, your market requires fast scaling. If your business operates in a winner-takes-all industry, you must act fast before competitors dominate the space. Secondly, you need capital-intensive infrastructure. Bootstrapping won't cut it if your startup requires factories, logistics or expensive research and development. Thirdly, you're willing to trade equity for speed. Making an investment means giving up a certain percentage of ownership. The trade-off for this? Faster execution, deeper talent pools and a competitive edge. But the ideal catch is that even if you raise money, think like a bootstrapped founder.

What is the most significant mistake founders make? They confuse raising money with success.

VC money is a loan, not a victory

When you take investor money, you've entered a contract—legally and strategically. Investors aren't donating cash. They expect returns, liquidity events, and growth on a scale. Many startups fail not because they didn't raise money but because they spent it too fast. Lesson? Fundraising is not an achievement—it's a responsibility.

Spend capital like it's your own money

The best founders treat investor money like their personal savings. Every rupee or dollar spent should serve a clear purpose—revenue growth, customer acquisition or product improvement.

How to Decide: Bootstrapping or Raising Capital?

Ask yourself these five questions:

- Can my business make money early on, or do I need upfront investment to survive? If yes, you should consider bootstrapping. If not, funding is the way to go.
- How fast do I need to grow? If you can afford slow growth, bootstrapping works. If speed is critical, funding is the way.
- Can I stay in control when raising money? If investors demand too much control, it may not be worth it.
- Is my industry capital-intensive? If yes, bootstrapping is unlikely to work.
- Do I have a clear plan for every dollar I raise? If you can't justify the spending, you don't need funding yet.

Funding Is a Tool, Not a Necessity

Bootstrapping and VC funding aren't opposing strategies; they are simply different ways of building a business. If you can build a sustainable, profitable business without external funding, it's always wise to do so. However, if your market requires rapid scaling and speed to remain competitive, raising capital becomes essential—but only if used strategically. Regardless of funding, every founder should operate with the discipline of a bootstrapped entrepreneur and ensure that every dollar is spent efficiently. Because ultimately success isn't defined by how much money you raise but by how effectively you manage and deploy the resources you have.

2.3 HOW TO PITCH AND WIN INVESTORS

Venture capitalists are not merely seeking novel ideas; they are discerning judges of your capacity to transform concepts into reality. A common pitfall for founders is mistaking their product as the focal point of their pitch. Investors are not captivated by the product itself but rather by its potential to solve a significant problem, its scalability, and your ability to establish market dominance.

The Anatomy of a Winning Pitch

To craft a compelling sales pitch, one that resonates with the astute investor, you must meticulously address the following elements:

1. **Problem:** Define the acute, pervasive problem you want to alleviate with your project. Investors seek solutions to substantial challenges that resonate with a broad audience and have a tangible impact.
2. **Solution:** Clearly articulate how your startup addresses this problem in a unique way that surpasses existing alternatives. Investors are drawn to solutions that are characterized by ingenuity, efficiency and a clear competitive advantage.
3. **Market opportunity:** Delineate the size and growth trajectory of the market your company is targeting. Investors are keen on ventures positioned to capture a significant share of a burgeoning market.
4. **Business model:** Elucidate your revenue generation strategy. Investors need to comprehend how your venture will transform its solution into a sustainable and profitable enterprise.

5. **Traction:** Present tangible evidence of your venture's early success. This can include paying customers, growth metrics, or a burgeoning community of early adopters. Investors want assurance that your venture is gaining momentum and resonating with its intended audience.
6. **Team:** Underscore why you and your team have the requisite skills, experience and unwavering commitment to navigate the inevitable challenges of entrepreneurship. Investors invest in people who exhibit the tenacity and vision to turn their aspirations into reality.
7. **The ask:** State clearly the amount of funding you are seeking and how it will be used judiciously to propel your venture. Investors need to align their investment with your strategic objectives and discern a clear path to growth and profitability.

Remember, investors are not swayed by mere possibilities; they seek ventures poised for inevitable success. Your pitch must transcend the realm of ideas and paint a vivid picture of a future reality that compels investors to become an integral part of your journey.

VC secret: Seasoned investors recognize that the ultimate investment is not solely the company itself but in the founders who propel it. By demonstrating profound understanding of the market, relentless execution and an unwavering vision, you will attract investment even if your product is not yet fully realized.

2.4 MANAGING RUNWAY AND BURN RATE

In the relentless pursuit of entrepreneurial triumph, one must not merely strive for growth but also for the unwavering endurance that precedes it. It is not the lack of innovation or ingenuity that spells the demise of a startup but the exhaustion of its financial lifeblood. The mismanagement of cash flow, like a silent assassin, has claimed more promising ventures than the fiercest competition.

A founder must navigate the treacherous tightrope between burning too fast and burning too slow, for both extremes can lead to ruin. To assume that a successful funding round guarantees a future of abundance is a perilous delusion. Markets shift like the tides, investors' priorities change like the wind, and growth without a sustainable revenue model is akin to building castles in the sand. Remember the cautionary tale of Housing.com, a once-promising startup that succumbed to the siren song of reckless spending, its coffers drained by lavish offices, excessive hiring and extravagant marketing campaigns. Funding, my fellow entrepreneurs, is not a licence for extravagance but a resource to be wielded with wisdom and foresight.

> Shreeram vividly recalls a particular startup that he had the opportunity to work with. They were driven, passionate, and brimming with innovative ideas. However, their financial situation was precarious, to say the least. They were burning through their seed funding at an alarming rate, and the spectre of failure loomed large.
>
> It was clear that drastic measures were needed. I introduced them to the concept of zero-based budgeting (ZBB).[10] It is a budgeting approach where every expense

must be justified from scratch in each new period, rather than basing budgets on prior year spending, promoting cost efficiency and strategic allocation of resources.

This approach, a stark departure from traditional budgeting methods, required them to justify every single expense from scratch, rather than simply relying on past budgets as a template. It was a challenging process, demanding a meticulous examination of every cost, every line item, and every financial decision.

But the results were nothing short of transformative. By meticulously scrutinizing their spending habits, they unearthed hidden inefficiencies, identified unnecessary costs, and discovered opportunities to reallocate resources more effectively. What initially seemed like a tedious exercise in financial discipline ultimately became a catalyst for strategic realignment and operational efficiency.

Through the diligent application of ZBB, they managed to significantly extend their runway, giving them the breathing room they desperately needed to refine their product, acquire new customers, and ultimately achieve profitability. It was a testament to the power of financial prudence, strategic planning, and the willingness to challenge conventional wisdom.

Conversely, to hoard one's capital, to fear the bold investment that fuels expansion, is to invite stagnation and surrender the field to one's rivals. Perplexity AI, a shining example of prudent growth, has demonstrated the power of strategic hiring and focused user acquisition, proving that measured investment can pave the path to sustainable success. Cash flow is the oxygen that sustains a venture, but excessive caution leads to suffocation.

Sridhar once worked with a promising startup that was champing at the bit to expand into new markets. Their enthusiasm was infectious, but they were a young company with limited resources, and he knew that a premature leap could overextend them. Sridhar advised them to take a step back and apply the principles of the lean startup methodology.[11]

The lean startup methodology is an approach to building businesses that emphasises rapid experimentation, validated learning, and iterative product development to reduce risk and build products that truly meet customer needs.

Instead of chasing growth at all costs, they focused on deeply understanding their core market. They ran a series of small, iterative experiments to test their assumptions and validate demand. They tweaked their product, their messaging, and their pricing, carefully measuring the impact of each change.

Through this process, they discovered a critical insight: a significant segment of their target audience was willing to pay a premium for a higher tier of service. This realization led them to restructure their pricing strategy and introduce a premium offering, which dramatically improved their unit economics and propelled them to profitability.

By first focusing on achieving sustainable growth in their core market, they built a solid foundation for expansion. They were no longer blindly throwing resources at new markets; they had the data and the financial stability to make informed decisions about where and how to expand. This disciplined approach allowed them to enter new markets strategically, with a clear understanding of their target customer and a validated business model.

The key takeaway? Sometimes, the smartest way to grow is to first focus on optimizing your existing business. By validating demand, refining your offering, and achieving profitability in your core market, you create a launchpad for sustainable expansion.

To extend your runway, to prolong your financial lifeline, is not to stifle growth but to cultivate it with strategic precision. Hire with discernment, for every new employee is a recurring expense that must be justified. Delay major expenditures until they are critical, for extravagance is a luxury that can be ill-afforded in the early stages of a venture. Seek out cost-effective growth channels, for organic traction is the bedrock of sustainable expansion. Prioritize revenue over funding, for customers are the ultimate investors in your vision. When you must seek funding, do so from a position of strength, with a clear path to profitability and a compelling narrative that resonates with investors.

Remember, my fellow entrepreneurs, your runway is your lifeline. Audit your burn rate, calculate your runway, and identify areas where you can trim expenses without compromising growth. If your runway is short, act decisively, for the only thing worse than running out of money is realizing it too late.

2.5 BUILDING A REVENUE MODEL THAT SUSTAINS GROWTH

In the relentless pursuit of entrepreneurial triumph, one must never lose sight of the paramount importance of building a robust revenue model. It is a grave error to fixate solely on raising capital, for the lifeblood of any enduring enterprise is the ability to generate a steady stream of revenue. The startups that stand the test of time are not those that rely on the fleeting sustenance of investor capital but those that construct a powerful revenue engine that fuels their growth.

Let us explore the two distinct paths that lie before you, the path of the triumph and the path of the builder. The triumph, ever seduced by the allure of external funding, treats fundraising as its sole business model. They chase investors with fervour, neglecting the cultivation of a loyal customer base. Their very existence hinges on securing the next round of funding, leaving them vulnerable to the vagaries of the investment climate. Like a house of cards, their enterprise collapses when the winds of fortune change.

Contrast this with the builder, who views funding as a strategic accelerant, not a lifeline. They prioritize profitability, scalability and sustainability, ensuring their business model is sound before seeking external capital. When they do raise funds, it is to propel an already thriving enterprise to new heights, not to merely keep the lights on.

The choice of revenue model is a pivotal one, for it determines how you generate income, scale your operations, and sustain growth. A misstep here can lead to a perilous depletion of resources, while the right model can pave the way to a predictable and high-margin business.

Consider the subscription model, favoured by many

software-as-a-service (SaaS) companies. By securing recurring revenue through monthly or annual subscriptions, they create a stable foundation for growth. This model fosters long-term customer relationships and ensures a consistent cash flow.

The marketplace model offers another compelling path to success. By connecting buyers and sellers and taking a commission on each transaction, these businesses can scale rapidly without the burdens of inventory management. They create an ecosystem where others transact, reaping the rewards of high margins without the risks associated with holding physical goods.

The freemium-to-paid model is a strategic approach that entices users with a free basic version while offering premium features for a fee. This allows businesses to build a broad user base and then convert a segment of those users into paying customers. The key is to provide genuine value upfront while ensuring the paid version offers compelling benefits that users find irresistible.

For those seeking high-ticket deals and long-term revenue streams, the enterprise sales model beckons. By selling expensive contracts to businesses, these startups secure substantial upfront payments and forge lasting relationships with their clients. While the number of customers may be smaller, the size of each deal and the resulting margins can be significant.

In the realm of pricing strategy, it is essential not to undervalue your offerings. Cheap pricing may attract a fleeting influx of customers, but it often comes at the cost of attracting the wrong kind of customers—those who churn quickly, demand excessive support, and are reluctant to upgrade. If your product or service is truly valuable, do not hesitate to charge accordingly. Customers who recognize its worth will be willing to pay a premium.

Consider the strategy of testing premium pricing. By setting your prices higher than your competitors, you signal the superior quality of your offerings, and filter out low-value customers. This approach can lead to higher margins and a more discerning clientele.

Another effective strategy is to start with a free version but limit access to certain features. This allows you to attract a wide audience while incentivizing users to upgrade to a paid plan for full functionality. The free version serves as a powerful hook, while the premium version offers the complete and irresistible experience.

The money game is not a matter of chance but of strategy. Startups that master the art of managing their finances survive and thrive, while those that neglect this crucial aspect falter and fade. Remember, survival is not merely about having a fantastic product; it's about generating revenue. Your technological marvel is meaningless if you cannot effectively sell it.

Understand your startup economics intimately. Know your customer acquisition cost, lifetime value, burn rate and runway. Without this knowledge, you are navigating blindly. Raise capital only when it is truly necessary, using it to fuel a proven model, not to prop up a failing one.

Master the art of pitching to investors. They invest in execution, not just ideas. If you cannot demonstrate traction and a clear path to profitability, you will struggle to secure funding. Control your burn rate with unwavering discipline. No matter how much capital you raise, operate with the frugality and resourcefulness of a bootstrapped founder.

The ultimate measure of success is not how much money you raise but how much money you earn. If your startup were to vanish tomorrow, would it leave a void in the market, or would customers simply move on? If your only plan is to perpetually chase the next funding round, you are one rejection away from collapse.

Investors, too, seek long-term viability. If your business model does not demonstrate a path to profitability, their interest will wane. Master the art of revenue generation, and you control your destiny. Ignore it, and even the most brilliant ideas will wither and die.

3

From Zero to Hundred: Marketing and Sales Foundations

Let it be understood, and etched into the very fabric of your ambition that your product cannot sell by itself however ingenious it may be. To believe otherwise is a fatal delusion, a pitfall that far too many founders plunge into, their dreams shattered upon the rocks of reality. They believe that the mere act of creation, the forging of a superior product, is sufficient. This is not the case. Even if your solution is a marvel of innovation, a beacon of progress, your venture is doomed to wither and perish if you neglect the vital art of sales. This is the crucible where the mettle of entrepreneurs is tested, where the weak falter and the strong prevail. They toil tirelessly, refining their creation, yet they shy away from the marketplace, the lifeblood of commerce. They build, they iterate, they refine, yet they fail to sell. It is sales that separate the titans from the shadows, the conquerors from the forgotten.

Observe the giants of the industry—Duolingo, Figma, Meesho, Notion and Revolut—what do they have in common?

They have mastered the art of customer acquisition through innovative, user-centred strategies. Rather than relying on traditional marketing, Duolingo has turned language learning into an addictive game, using streaks and leaderboards to drive engagement and retention. Figma disrupted the design industry by making collaborative design seamless, first by winning over designers and letting word-of-mouth fuel its rapid expansion. Meesho tapped into India's social commerce boom by empowering small entrepreneurs, enabling millions to start their online businesses with zero investment. Notion built a devoted user base without heavy advertising, by leveraging community-driven content, turning everyday users into brand evangelists.

Revolut, a UK-based fintech disruptor, revolutionized banking by offering fee-free currency exchange, crypto trading and personalized financial services, attracting young, global-minded consumers who wanted more control over their money. The lesson is clear: Customer acquisition isn't just about marketing; it's about creating products so compelling that the users themselves become the biggest growth engine.

3.1 THE ART OF PERSUASION AND EARLY SALES

Let us dispel a most dangerous illusion: the notion that a superior product sells itself. Nothing could be further from the truth. In the realm of entrepreneurship, the ability to persuade, to instill belief, is paramount. If your venture cannot ignite the spark of conviction in the hearts of your potential customers, it shall wither and fail, regardless of the brilliance of your creation. Observe the titans of industry; each, without exception, possessed the gift of selling. Henry Ford sold the promise of affordable automobiles to the masses with his revolutionary assembly line long before the Model T, a car manufactured by the Ford Motor Company from 1908 to 1927, considered the first mass-produced, affordable automobile which made car ownership accessible to the middle class; it was designed by Henry Ford and is often referred to as the 'Tin Lizzie' due to its simple design and widespread popularity.

Elon Musk sold the dream of sustainable energy and space exploration with his bold vision long before Tesla and Space Exploration Technologies Corp—commonly referred to as SpaceX—reshaped their respective industries.

However, selling is not manipulation. Rather, it is the art of solving a problem so profoundly that your customers feel compelled to acquire your solution. The psychology of early sales is rooted in a simple truth: People do not merely buy products; they invest in solutions, emotions and identities.

First, consider the distinction between painkillers and vitamins. Painkillers address urgent, acute needs, while vitamins are merely supplementary. In the entrepreneurial arena, your initial offering must be a painkiller. Headspace, a mental health app and website that offers guided meditations, sleep sounds and coaching, offered a solution to the growing problem of stress and anxiety in modern life. Slack, a cloud-based messaging app that helps businesses communicate and collaborate, addressed the frustration of inefficient communication within teams. While a new productivity app is beneficial, it lacks the urgency of a true painkiller.

Second, remember that people buy aspirations, not just products. Great brands sell transformations. GoPro, a US-based company that manufactures action cameras, mobile apps and video-editing software, sells not just cameras but the dream of capturing and sharing life's adventures. Peloton, a fitness company that sells fitness equipment and offers live and on-demand fitness classes, doesn't just offer stationary bikes—it sells a vision of community, fitness and personal achievement. Thus, your startup must also sell a vision of a better future.

Third, recognize that trust precedes transactions. Before a customer parts with their hard-earned money, they must trust you. Social proof in the form of early testimonials fosters confidence. Scarcity and exclusivity, as demonstrated by luxury brands like Rolex, a Swiss watchmaker that designs and manufactures luxury watches, heighten demand. Early evangelists, such as the passionate users who championed the early days of Reddit, an American social network for news aggregation, content rating and creating forums, are invaluable in generating organic growth.

> Sridhar recalls a brilliant engineer he once mentored. The entrepreneur had poured his heart and soul into developing truly groundbreaking water purification technology, a marvel of ingenuity that held the potential to transform lives. Yet, for all his technical prowess, he faltered when it came to articulating the value of his creation to potential investors and customers. He was essentially a master of innovation but a novice in communication.
>
> Recognizing his struggle, Sridhar introduced him to the problem–agitate–solution framework (PAS),[12] a persuasive communication technique that has proven its efficacy time and again. The PAS framework is a persuasive communication technique that involves identifying a problem, intensifying the emotional impact of that problem, and then offering a solution to resolve it.

> Sridhar guided him to shift his messaging, to begin by highlighting the customer's pain point—the pervasive issue of contaminated water. We then emphasised the dire consequences of inaction—the health risks, the financial burden, and the sheer inconvenience of relying on subpar solutions. Finally, we presented his technology as the ultimate solution, articulating its benefits in clear, concise and compelling language.
>
> This subtle shift in communication strategy proved to be a game-changer. Armed with a newfound clarity of messaging, the engineer confidently approached potential investors, painting a vivid picture of the problem, agitating their concerns, and ultimately presenting his technology as the definitive answer. The result was nothing short of transformative. He secured his first major deal, attracting the funding needed to scale his operations and bring his life-changing innovation to the masses.

Your First Sales Matter More than Anything Else

Your initial customers are not mere transactions; they validate your business model. Razorpay, in its nascent stages, focused on convincing a select group of businesses of the superiority of its payment processing solution, and through their success, the word spread. Similarly, Ola prioritized the satisfaction of its earliest customers, which led to exponential growth through word of mouth. The formula is clear: Sell directly and personally to your first users, demonstrate the superiority of your product, and iterate based on their feedback. If you cannot persuade ten people, you will never persuade ten thousand.

Shreeram once had the opportunity to consult with a fledgling startup that was developing a new type of baby monitor. The founders, brimming with passion and enthusiasm for their innovative product, had poured their hearts and souls into its creation. Despite their best efforts, however, sales remained stubbornly stagnant. They found themselves trapped in the all-too-common entrepreneurial dilemma: a fantastic product that no one seemed to want.

Observing their predicament, Shreeram introduced them to a powerful concept known as the jobs-to-be-done (JTBD) framework.[13]

The jobs-to-be-done framework is a customer-centred approach that focuses on understanding the underlying 'job' or outcome that customers are trying to achieve when they hire a product or service to solve a specific problem.

This approach emphasises the importance of understanding the underlying 'job' for which customers 'hire' a product. It shifts the focus from the product's features and functionalities to the deeper needs and motivations of the customer.

In the case of the baby monitor, the founders had emphasised the technical specifications—the crystal-clear video quality, the advanced motion detection features and the user-friendly interface. While these features were undoubtedly impressive, they failed to resonate with the target audience.

Applying the jobs-to-be-done framework, we delved into the minds of parents, seeking to understand their core desires. We discovered that what parents truly craved was not just a baby monitor; they craved peace of mind, the assurance that their child was safe and sound, and perhaps most importantly, the ability to get a good night's sleep.

Armed with this insight, the founders revamped their marketing strategy. They repositioned their messaging to highlight how their baby monitor could help parents achieve those elusive hours of uninterrupted sleep. They addressed the anxieties and concerns of parents, assuring them that their product would provide them with the vigilance and reassurance they needed to finally rest easy.

The results were remarkable. By aligning their product with the deeper emotional needs of their customers, the founders unlocked a surge in demand. Sales soared, and the once struggling startup embarked on a path of rapid growth and success.

This experience served as a powerful reminder that innovation is not merely about creating new products or technologies; it is about understanding the human needs that drive customer behaviour. By embracing the jobs-to-be-done framework, entrepreneurs can unlock a profound understanding of their target audience and position their products in a way that resonates with their deepest desires.

How to Win Early Sales: The 3-Step Playbook

First, solve an obvious and urgent problem. If extensive explanations are required, the problem is not significant enough. Zoom, for instance, addressed the need for easy and reliable video conferencing, particularly during the rise of remote working. Instacart, an American delivery company based in San Francisco that operates grocery delivery and pickup services in the United States and Canada, tackled the challenge of delivering groceries conveniently for busy people. Make your value proposition immediately apparent.

Second, sell before you build. Your startup is not a mere hobby; it must generate revenue. For example, Minecraft, a 2011 sandbox game developed and published by Swedish video game developer Mojang Studios, started with a basic version that garnered early adopters and generated revenue before expanding its features. Buffer, one of the best-known social media marketing tools serving small businesses, creators and individuals, gained initial traction with a simple social media scheduling tool before developing a full suite of marketing solutions. Your product is not validated until someone is willing to pay for it.

Third, understand that early sales are the founder's responsibility. Marc Benioff's Salesforce (a cloud-based customer relationship management [CRM] platform that helps businesses manage customer data, sales and marketing), Whitney Wolfe Herd's Bumble (a free dating app and social network that helps people find matches, make friends and network), and Reshma Saujani's Girls Who Code (an international nonprofit that aims to increase the number of women in computer science) have all actively engaged with early customers and built relationships to drive initial growth. If you believe you are 'not a salesperson', your venture is doomed.

What Founders Get Wrong about Sales

Many founders overcomplicate their messaging, struggle with direct sales, and waste time perfecting a product without validating demand. A perfect product without customers is worthless.

Selling is your startup's lifeline

A startup's success hinges on the founder's mastery of persuasion and early sales. Be direct, be relentless, and be obsessed. Your startup's future resides not in code or business models but in your ability to convince the world of your product's worth.

> Sridhar once had the pleasure of advising a fledgling startup on the cusp of launching a new online course. The founders, brilliant minds in their respective fields, were brimming with enthusiasm and eager to share their expertise with the world. However, they had overlooked a crucial element in their marketing strategy: the power of social proof.
>
> They had no testimonials from previous students, no evidence to demonstrate the effectiveness of their course. Sridhar suggested a simple yet effective solution: create a pilot programme and offer it to a select group of beta testers in exchange for their honest feedback and, if warranted, testimonials.
>
> The founders embraced this strategy, and the results were remarkable. The beta testers, thrilled with the quality of the course and the expertise of the instructors, gave glowing testimonials that became the cornerstone of the startup's marketing efforts. Armed with this social proof, the founders were able to confidently launch their course to a wider audience, achieving significant success.
>
> This experience reinforced a fundamental principle of entrepreneurship: validation is paramount. Before investing substantial resources in developing a product or service, it is essential to gather evidence that it resonates with your target audience and fulfils a genuine need.

3.2 FINDING YOUR FIRST 100 CUSTOMERS

Let it be known, my friends, that many a promising venture has withered not because of a flawed creation but because of a fatal ignorance of how to attract its initial devotees. Your first hundred customers are not just transactions; they are the bedrock on which your empire shall stand. They are the proof of concept, your invaluable feedback mechanism, and the earliest evangelists of your vision. They are the ones who will illuminate the path, revealing what flourishes and what falters, what must be altered before you dare to scale. This is not a matter of chance but of strategic mastery. Approach this endeavour with a keen mind and a relentless spirit, and you shall swiftly discover them and convert them effectively.

Where to Find the First 100 Customers?

Do not delude yourself into believing these precious individuals will materialize by mere wishful thinking. You must seek them out with unwavering determination and imbue them with your vision. Here is how you can proceed:

1. Start with your network: If you can't sell to people you know, you can't sell at all

Many a founder, blinded by vanity, dismisses his or her immediate network, believing that true success lies only in conquering strangers. This is a grave error. True momentum is often ignited by the spark of personal connections. Observe the rise of Calendly, a cloud-based app that helps users schedule meetings and appointments. Tope Awotona first introduced this scheduling automation platform to his network of contacts, leveraging their trust and feedback to fuel early growth. Consider the trajectory of Superhuman, a private company that offers an email app and AI-powered tools to help users be more productive. The email productivity tool, which Rahul Vohra strategically seeded within his network of high-performing individuals, sparked a wave of adoption through word-of-mouth referrals.

If you cannot persuade those who know you, who have witnessed your journey and believe in your potential, how can you ever hope to sway the hearts and minds of strangers? Start your outreach with the familiar—friends, colleagues and LinkedIn (a social networking platform for professionals to connect, share information, and build their careers and connections within the industry). Tap into the power of startup and alumni networks where your credibility is already established. Engage them directly, solicit their candid feedback, and make them your first paying disciples, your earliest champions in the marketplace. For it is these initial sparks of conviction that will ultimately ignite the flame for widespread adoption.

Shreeram once had the pleasure of mentoring a brilliant woman who was passionate about developing a new line of organic skincare products. She had poured her heart and soul into developing unique formulations, using only the finest natural ingredients. However, like many first-time entrepreneurs, she was hesitant to share her creations with the world. She feared rejection, worried that her network would not appreciate the value of her products.

Shreeram encouraged her to embrace the principles of the lean startup methodology, emphasising the importance of validating demand early on. Shreeram suggested she start by creating a minimum viable product (MVP)—a small batch of her most promising products—and share these with her friends and family. Essentially, Shreeram urged her to treat her inner circle as her first test market.

To her delight, her friends and family not only embraced her products with open arms but also gave her invaluable feedback. They shared their honest opinions about the texture, scent and overall effectiveness of the products, helping her identify areas for improvement. Their enthusiastic support led to the first sales, providing her the validation and confidence she needed to take the next step.

Armed with this initial feedback and fuelled by the encouragement of her early adopters, she refined her formulations, tweaked her packaging, and gradually expanded her reach. What started as a tentative experiment within her network blossomed into a thriving business built on a foundation of validated demand and customer focus.

2. Be active in relevant online communities: Fish where the fish are

To build in isolation is to build in vain. You must venture where your audience already congregates and engage with them. Look at how Airtable, a cloud-based platform that combines spreadsheet functionality with database, and Brex61, a financial technology (fintech) company that offers business banking, expense management and credit cards, gained early traction on Reddit, Twitter and Product Hunt, answering queries, solving problems and granting early access.

One can look at real estate company Opendoor's strategic targeting of online real estate forums and American tech company Ripple's (an American technology company, which offers enterprise blockchain products on the XRP Ledger and other networks) CEO Brad Garlinghouse, who cultivated a Twitter (X)—a social media platform that allows users to send and receive short messages called tweets—following years before launch. Find these vibrant communities and embed yourself in them. Engage in discussions on LinkedIn and Twitter; answer questions on Reddit, a social news website and online forum where users can share and discuss content, and Quora, a social media platform that allows users to ask and answer questions on a variety of topics; launch on Product Hunt and join relevant Facebook and WhatsApp groups. Remember to add value before you seek to extract it.

Sridhar once had the opportunity to collaborate with a fledgling startup that was developing a cutting-edge productivity app. The founders, a dynamic duo with a passion for efficiency and a knack for community building, embraced a novel approach known as 'building in public'.[14]

Building in public is a transparent approach where founders openly share their startup's journey, progress and challenges with the public to build trust, gather feedback and foster a community of early supporters.

They eschewed the traditional secrecy that often shrouds startups in their early stages, opting instead for radical transparency. They actively documented their progress, shared their challenges, and solicited feedback from potential users in various online productivity communities.

This approach proved to be remarkably effective. By engaging with their target audience early and often, the founders cultivated a loyal following of individuals who felt invested in the app's success. They fostered a sense of trust and transparency, creating a community of early adopters who were eager to provide valuable feedback and contribute to the app's development.

When the app was finally launched, the founders were not met with indifference or scepticism but with a ready-made audience, a community of enthusiastic users who had been eagerly anticipating the release. The app's launch was not just a product release but a celebration of a collective effort, a testament to the power of community and transparency on the entrepreneurial journey.

3. Leverage industry events and niche meetups: Early customers trust real interactions

Trust is earned most swiftly through direct and personal engagement—attending events, speaking at meetups, and meeting your potential customers face to face. Look at Zerodha's founder Nithin Kamath, who built trust within trader communities, and Airbnb's founders, who went door to door in New York. Consider Tesla's impact at industry expos. Seek out conferences, trade shows and meetups within your niche and present yourself where your customers reside.

4. Cold outreach and direct selling: Don't wait—find them

Do not sit idly by, waiting for customers to appear. Approach them, one by one, and demonstrate the superiority of your solution. Girish Mathrubootham of Freshworks won his first customers through cold emails, and Razorpay won over customers through direct emails and personal demonstrations. The founders of Airbnb wrote to thousands of hosts. Craft compelling subject lines, personalize each message, be concise, and follow up relentlessly. If your offer fails to elicit a response, strengthen your pitch.

5. Give people a reason to talk about you: Create viral loops

Word of mouth remains the most powerful catalyst for growth. To leverage it, businesses must incentivize referrals, simplify sharing, and engage highly active users. Think of the Cash App, which skyrocketed in popularity through referral bonuses that rewarded both the inviter and the invitee. Duolingo turned language learning into a social habit, encouraging users to challenge their friends and maintain streaks. Robinhood, in its early days, offered exclusive early access to its trading platform to users who had referred others, creating viral momentum. If your first hundred customers each bring in two more, you've built a self-sustaining growth engine.

> Sridhar recalls working with a fledgling startup that was on the cusp of launching a novel subscription box service. They were eager to make a splash in the market and sought my advice on how it could achieve rapid growth. Sridhar recommended implementing a referral programme, one that would incentivize their early adopters to become enthusiastic evangelists for their brand.
>
> The strategy was simple yet elegant. Customers who already experienced the delight of receiving their curated subscription boxes were offered a generous bonus for every new subscriber they brought on board. To further amplify the programme's reach, we made it incredibly easy for these satisfied customers to share their unique referral links across their social media channels.
>
> The results were nothing short of remarkable. Each new subscriber, enthralled by the service and incentivized

by the referral programme, became a conduit for further growth, creating a self-perpetuating cycle of customer acquisition. The initial trickle of customers soon turned into a torrent, propelling the startup to exponential growth. It was a testament to the power of harnessing the enthusiasm of your most loyal customers and turning them into passionate advocates for your brand.

Your First 100 Customers Define Everything

They validate your idea, shape your product roadmap, and lay the foundation for scaling. Finding them is not a matter of luck but of unwavering execution. If you cannot find a hundred willing buyers, you will never find a thousand. Master early sales, outreach and engagement, and you will build a community of loyal advocates who will propel your startup to greatness.

3.3 DIGITAL GROWTH: SEO, SOCIAL MEDIA AND PAID ADVERTISEMENTS

A decade ago, the seeds of startup success were sown in the fertile ground of word of mouth, nurtured by media coverage, and transplanted through offline referrals. But let us be clear: the landscape has shifted irrevocably. Today, in the digital age, if your enterprise lacks a vibrant, visible presence in the online realm, it's as if it does not exist. The internet, the great democratizer, has levelled the playing field, allowing startups, even those with meagre marketing budgets, to rise above the industry giants through the strategic application of search engine optimization (SEO), mastery of social media, and judicious use of paid advertising. Master these digital growth principles, and you can liberate yourself from the shackles of traditional advertising, creating a self-perpetuating engine of demand.

Search Engine Optimization (SEO): Winning Organic Growth

Startups that truly understand the power of SEO wield an unparalleled advantage, achieving dominance in their industries without relying on constant ad spends. Consider NerdWallet, a personal finance company that helps users make financial decisions and has built an empire in the personal finance space by creating highly optimized, educational content that ranks for top financial queries. Notion's SEO-driven guides and templates attract millions of users searching for productivity solutions. Calendly, rather than pouring money into ads, mastered search intent by optimizing content around scheduling-related queries, ensuring it's the go-to solution for professionals. To win in SEO, you must first embrace search intent—customers don't search for your startup, they search for solutions. If someone looks up 'best productivity tools for remote teams,' your platform must be the first one they see. Understand your audience's search behaviour and craft content that positions your startup as the inevitable answer.

Sridhar remembers working with this ambitious startup that was developing a cutting-edge CRM specifically designed for small businesses. They had a fantastic product, but they were struggling to gain traction organically. Their website was buried deep in the search results, and their organic traffic was practically non-existent.

So Sridhar introduced them to the topic cluster model,[15] a powerful SEO framework that emphasises structured content and internal linking. They brainstormed together and decided to create a comprehensive pillar page focused on 'effective CRM strategies for small businesses'. This pillar page served as the central hub, linking a series of in-depth blog posts that addressed specific pain points and challenges faced by small businesses when it came to managing customer relationships.

The results were remarkable. Search engine rankings climbed steadily, and their organic traffic saw a significant increase. The topic cluster model had not only improved their website's visibility but also established them as thought leaders in the small business CRM space.

Second, create evergreen, high-value content. Educational content is the currency of the digital age. Write blog posts, guides and case studies that solve problems. Use keywords naturally, eschewing keyword stuffing, and always prioritize user experience. Remember, consistency is paramount. SEO is a long-term investment, but the compounding effect is a force to be reckoned with.

Sridhar once had the pleasure of advising a fledgling startup on the launch of its new online course. The company was eager to make a splash in the crowded online education market but was also acutely aware of the challenges involved in attracting and converting customers. Sridhar suggested they leverage the power of the content marketing funnel,[16] a strategy that involves creating a series of increasingly targeted content pieces designed to guide potential customers through the buyer's journey.

The content marketing funnel is a strategic model that outlines the stages of a customer's journey from awareness to purchase, emphasising the creation and distribution of relevant content to engage and nurture leads at each stage.

They began by crafting a high-value, comprehensive guide that served as a free lead magnet. This top-of-funnel content was strategically distributed across various online channels to raise awareness about the company and share its expertise. This attracted a steady stream of organic traffic, nurtured the trust of their target audience, and most importantly, captured email addresses.

Armed with a growing list of subscribers, they then deployed a series of carefully crafted email sequences and retargeting campaigns. These initiatives delivered a consistent flow of value-driven content, solidifying their authority and building a strong rapport with their audience. Finally, after weeks of nurturing and engagement, they presented their paid course, positioning it as a natural next step for those seeking to deepen their knowledge and skills.

The results were impressive. The combination of high-quality content, strategic distribution and targeted nurturing led to a significant increase in course enrolments. The startup had effectively transformed casual visitors into paying customers, demonstrating the power of a well-executed content marketing strategy.

Third, optimize your landing pages. Ensure that your homepage, product pages and blogs are all SEO-friendly. Craft compelling meta descriptions, headers and structured data to enhance discoverability. Speed and mobile friendliness are non-negotiable; a sluggish website is a death knell for conversions. SEO is the most cost-effective long-term growth strategy. Begin early, and you shall own the search traffic while your competitors squander their resources on fleeting advertisements.

> Shreeram once had the pleasure of mentoring a brilliant young woman who was on the cusp of launching a sustainable clothing line. She had poured her heart and soul into designing a collection of garments that were not only stylish and ethically produced but also environmentally responsible. However, when it came to marketing her brand, she hesitated. Social media, with its relentless demands for attention and often superficial nature, seemed antithetical to the values she held dear.
>
> Shreeram recognized her apprehension and introduced her to Simon Sinek's Golden Circle framework,[17] a business model that emphasises the 'why' (purpose), followed by 'how' (process), and then 'what' (product or service), to inspire action and create a deeper connection with the audience.
>
> Shreeram encouraged her to share her passion for sustainability, articulate her mission and the profound reasons for her entrepreneurial pursuit, and let her authentic voice shine through.
>
> She took the advice to heart and began crafting compelling narratives that resonated with her target audience. She spoke about the environmental impact of fast fashion, the exploitation of workers in traditional garment factories, and her unwavering commitment to creating a better world through conscious consumerism.

She talked about the stories behind her designs, the meticulous sourcing of sustainable materials, and the ethical manufacturing processes she had painstakingly implemented.

The response was remarkable. Her genuine storytelling, devoid of marketing gimmicks and sales pitches, struck a chord with consumers who were eager to support businesses that aligned with their values. She cultivated a loyal following of customers who not only admired her products but also believed in her mission. Her social media channels became a platform for meaningful conversations, a space where like-minded people could connect and share their passion for sustainability.

This experience reinforced my belief in the power of authentic storytelling. When entrepreneurs lead with their 'why' when they share their passion and purpose, they create a powerful connection with their audience that transcends the transactional nature of business. They build brands that are not merely defined by their products or services, but by the values they represent and the positive impact they want to create.

Social Media and Virality: Building a Startup That Markets Itself

Social media is not merely a platform for posting updates; it is a powerful lever for distribution. The startups that truly flourish treat social media as a formidable growth engine. Consider Daniel Ek, the founder of Spotify, a music and podcast streaming service that lets you listen to millions of songs and podcasts. The platform has strategically leveraged its public presence and industry insights to position Spotify as a dominant force in music streaming. Then there is the example of Vinted, an online marketplace for buying and selling second-hand items, the European second-hand fashion marketplace, which harnessed the power of community-driven content on Instagram, a social media app that allows users to share photos and videos, and TikTok, a social media app that lets users create, share and discover short videos, to grow a loyal seller and buyer base. Klarna, a 'buy now, pay later' (BNPL) service, allows customers to split purchases into multiple payments, and has established itself as a fintech giant in Europe through collaboration with influencers and meme-driven marketing.

To harness the power of social media, you should first cultivate a founder-led brand. People trust people more than brands. Share insights, behind-the-scenes glimpses and lessons learnt; authenticity resonates. Second, engage in communities. Don't just merely post; interact. The most potent growth stems not from broadcasting about your startup but from actively contributing to conversations. Engage in Twitter threads, LinkedIn discussions, Reddit forums and Slack groups. Answer questions, provide value, and establish yourself as an authority. Third, make your product inherently shareable. Virality is not a matter of chance; it's engineered. Notion's free templates and Zoom's one-click invite links facilitated widespread adoption without the need for advertisements. Incentivize users to share—referral bonuses, social rewards and community-building features.

Remember, social media is not about posting content, it is about initiating conversations.

Paid Advertising: The Right Way to Do It

Startups often squander millions on advertisements that yield no conversions, mistakenly believing that spending equals growth. Paid acquisition should amplify organic growth, not replace it.

Consider the examples of Zomato, a restaurant aggregator and food delivery company that helps users find restaurants, order food and read reviews, and Swiggy, an online food ordering and delivery company based in Bengaluru, India, which have mastered hyper-targeted local ads to acquire users efficiently. Tesla, which barely spends on advertisements, relies instead on organic demand and public relations to drive sales. Airbnb employed precision-targeted ads only after perfecting its referral strategy. To advertise without burning money, start small, optimize and scale. Do not blindly pour money into advertisements without rigorously testing messaging, audience and conversion rates. Run micro-campaigns to identify what resonates and then double down on what works. Second, employ retargeting to capture the visitors who did not convert. Most users will not make a purchase on their initial visit. Facebook and Google retargeting keep your brand top of mind until they are ready to buy. Third, blend paid and organic advertising. If you rely solely on advertising, you are merely renting customers. By building organic traffic, you own them. The most successful startups use paid advertisements to amplify organic content, not supplant it.

Digital growth is about leverage, not mere expenditure. Many founders squander time on social media without understanding the mechanics of growth. Others burn through capital on advertisements without a sustainable acquisition strategy. The most effective digital growth strategies are those that leverage SEO to fuel long-term traffic and credibility, social media to create brand momentum and virility, and paid advertisements to amplify what is already working. The winning startups don't just spend money on marketing; they engineer sustainable, scalable and cost-efficient digital growth engines. Their job is not merely to attract attention but to convert that attention into customers. Master digital growth, and you will require neither luck nor excessive funding; your startup will grow on autopilot.

3.4 STORYTELLING AND BRANDING FOR STARTUPS

The true architects of success, the founders who etch their names in the annals of industry, are not just builders of products but master storytellers. Understand this: A startup's victory is forged not solely by the mechanics of its creation but by the compelling narratives it weaves.

A superior product, shackled by a feeble brand, will falter, while a potent brand can command the marketplace even with a moderately adequate offering. The clamour of competition is deafening, a cacophony of advertisements, influencer endorsements and public relations blitzes. Yet, true branding is not about contributing to the noise; it is about cultivating resonance. Your startup will endure if it becomes ingrained in the collective memory. It will flourish if it engenders unwavering belief. It will attain iconic status if it becomes the subject of ceaseless conversation. This chapter is therefore dedicated to mastering storytelling, the art of crafting a brand that endures, attracting customers, galvanizing employees, and cultivating a loyal following that transcends fleeting trends.

People Don't Buy What You Do. They Buy Why You Do It

The graveyard of failed startups is populated by those who erred in their focus. They mistook branding for a mere assemblage of logos, colours and advertisements. This is a grave miscalculation. Branding, in its essence, is about meaning. It is the intangible feeling that arises when your name is spoken. It is the reason Tesla is not merely a purveyor of automobiles, and Nike, a global company that designs and sells athletic shoes, apparel and sports equipment, is not simply a manufacturer of footwear. Great brands answer a fundamental question: Why should anyone care? Remember, people do not purchase what you do; they purchase why you do it. Should your narrative be forgettable, your startup will likely be as well. Consider Ather Energy, an Indian company that designs and manufactures electric scooters in India. The company didn't simply produce an electric scooter; they ignited a movement centred on sustainable, intelligent transportation. Its story was not about selling a vehicle but about revolutionizing urban mobility. The branding positioned the company as the Apple of electric scooters: clean, premium and futuristic. Instead of relying on conventional marketing tactics, they nurtured an engaged community of tech-savvy, eco-conscious buyers. Ather's story was not about scooters; it was about a cleaner, brighter future, and that narrative forged a cult-like customer base.

How to Create a Brand That Sticks

Were your startup to vanish tomorrow, would its absence be noted? A robust brand does more than simplify marketing; it cultivates customer loyalty and employee motivation, and renders competitors inconsequential.

To construct a brand that withstands the test of time, adhere to these principles.

1. Clarity over complexity

Your message must be so simple that a five-year-old could articulate it. Domino's did not burden their audience with convoluted explanations of high-quality ingredients and efficient delivery. They declared, '30 minutes or it's free'. A brand that is difficult to explain is a brand that is easily dismissed. Take the example of Wise (formerly TransferWise), a financial services company that allows users to send and receive money internationally. In a financial world cluttered with hidden fees and slow international transfers, they offered 'Money without borders—fast, low-cost international transfers.' They chose to compete for simplicity, not complexity. Their brand promise was clear, and their execution solidified their position as the go-to platform for international money transfers. Remember, if your value is hard to explain, your brand is hard to remember.

> Shreeram once worked with a financial planning startup that was struggling to gain traction. Their brand message was convoluted and failed to resonate with their target audience. They had a great product, but they weren't communicating its value effectively. He decided to apply the AIDA mode—attention, interest, desire, action—to streamline their messaging.
>
> First, Shreeram grabbed the attention of the audience by leading with a simple, relatable problem statement: 'Tired of feeling lost and confused when it comes to

managing your finances?' This immediately struck a chord with people who were struggling to navigate the complexities of personal finance.

Next, Shreeram piqued their interest by highlighting the unique features of the startup's platform, such as its AI-powered financial advisor and personalized investment recommendations. This showcased the innovative technology behind the solution and how it could benefit users.

To create desire, Shreeram showcased testimonials and success stories from satisfied customers who had achieved their financial goals using the platform. This provided social proof and demonstrated the tangible value of the service.

Finally, Shreeram included a clear call to action, urging potential users to sign up for a free trial or schedule a consultation. This made it easy for interested individuals to take the next step and engage with the startup.

The results were remarkable. The streamlined messaging resonated with potential users, leading to a significant increase in signups and engagement. Moreover, the clear and concise communication of the startup's value proposition instilled confidence in investors, paving the way for successful funding rounds. This experience reinforced the power of the AIDA model in crafting compelling brand narratives that drive both customer acquisition and investor interest.

2. Design matters—because people feel before they think

Your design is your brand's visual voice. Before customers hear your pitch or use your product, they see you. A cheap aesthetic implies a cheap product. A slow and clunky website suggests a slow and clunky business. Conversely, beauty implies value. People respond to design emotionally, not analytically. Take Figma, whose design felt revolutionary. Their clean, modern user interface made traditional software seem outdated. Real-time collaboration fostered a sense of belonging to a new era of design. Figma's success was rooted in its futuristic appearance, a promise that was reinforced at every touchpoint. Your product's first impression is your brand's first impression.

> Sridhar worked with a promising e-commerce startup. They had a fantastic product, but their website was a mess. It was like a maze with no clear path, and the design looked like it was from the dial-up era. He could see they were losing potential customers left and right.
>
> So Sridhar rolled up his sleeves and put on a CRO hat. He started with A/B testing,[18] experimenting with different layouts and calls to action.
>
> A/B testing is a randomized experimentation method that compares two or more versions of a website, app or marketing asset to determine which performs better, based on specific metrics like conversion rates.
>
> He streamlined the checkout process, making it as smooth as butter. He gave the user interface a much-needed facelift, removing all the clunky elements that were causing friction.
>
> The results were like night and day. The startup's conversion rates shot up, and sales saw a significant boost. It was a real testament to the power of CRO and a reminder that even the best products can fail if the user experience isn't up to par.

3. Brand consistency: Every touchpoint matters

Your brand extends beyond your logo—it encompasses your website, customer support, email responses, social media presence and even product packaging. It is what people say about you when you are not present. Inconsistency breeds distrust. Apple's branding is uniform across all platforms, reinforcing its sleek, premium image. The same is the case with Boat, an Indian consumer electronics company that sells audio products, smartwatches and other accessories. As India's leading audio and lifestyle brand, it ensures a bold, youth-centred experience across its website, influencer campaigns and product packaging, creating an aspirational identity. Man Matters, a digital health and men's wellness platform offering products and consultations, built its reputation through sleek design, transparent communication and high-quality content, ensuring every customer touchpoint feels personalized and premium. Every interaction should reinforce your brand's core values—disconnected experiences erode trust. Every customer interaction should feel like a continuation of the same story.

4. Make your brand a movement, not just a business

Powerful brands sell belonging, not just products. The Souled Store, an online shop that sells pop-culture-inspired clothing, accessories and merchandise, is not just about apparel; it is a celebration of pop culture and fandom. Sugar Cosmetics, a cruelty-free makeup brand that offers products for eyes, lips, face and nails, stands not only for beauty products but also for fearless self-expression and individuality. Sleepy Owl Coffee, an Indian coffee brand that sells a variety of coffee products including instant coffee, cold brew and hot brew, is more than just a D2C coffee brand—it embodies the craft coffee revolution in India, bringing an artisanal experience to home brews. The Ken, a subscription-based premium journalism service focused on quality long-form content, has transformed business journalism into an engaged community by making readers feel part of an elite, well-informed circle.

Great brands build an identity, not just a business. The more your customers see themselves in your brand, the stronger and more unshakeable your startup becomes.

Branding Is an Investment, Not an Expense

Many founders treat branding as an afterthought, believing a great product will suffice. This is a fatal mistake. A great product without a strong brand remains a secret, and secrets don't scale. Your brand is the bedrock of growth. It makes your startup memorable, desirable and defensible. Effective branding reduces acquisition costs, fosters customer loyalty and attracts top talent.

Failure to brand effectively consigns you to a perpetual struggle for attention. Mastering it will have people lining up to join your movement. So the question is, what story will your startup tell?

3.5 BUILDING A COMMUNITY AROUND YOUR PRODUCT

Understand this, my friend: Startups that forge unbreakable communities are the architects of enduring triumph. Mere customers are fleeting; it is the creation of devoted fans that secures your legacy.

Witness the power of exclusivity as CureFit, a health and fitness platform that offers online and offline services, has done, transforming fitness from a service into a lifestyle movement where members feel not just like customers but part of an elite, health-conscious tribe. Pharmeasy, an online healthcare marketplace that connects patients with pharmacies and diagnostic centres, has not only sold medicines online but also built a trusted healthcare ecosystem where users feel secure and empowered in managing their wellbeing. Then there is Headspace, which engaged millions in the mindfulness and mental wellness revolution by turning meditation into a daily ritual rather than just an app feature.

These examples are not mere coincidences but blueprints for your own success.

How to Build a Community That Sells for You

Embrace the power of user-generated content. Allow your customers to become your storytellers, crafting reviews, tutorials and testimonials. This is free, potent marketing—a testament to the authentic value you provide. Extend the privilege of exclusive access to your early adopters, those who yearn to feel like insiders. Grant them beta access, bestow upon them special perks, and treat them as VIPs. They will become your most loyal advocates.

Shreeram once had the pleasure of mentoring a bright young founder who was developing a fitness app. He was a firm believer in the power of social engagement and wanted to leverage it to drive user retention. He had cleverly designed his app based on Nir Eyal's hook model[19]—a framework for building habit-forming products.

Nir Eyal's hook model is a behavioural framework that outlines how successful products drive user engagement through a cycle of trigger, action, variable reward and investment, ultimately forming habitual user behaviour.

The app prompted users to share their workout routines and progress photos on social media. This seemingly simple act triggered a powerful cycle of engagement. The app's prompts acted as a trigger, persuading the user to take action. Sharing on social media was followed by the variable reward of likes and comments. Finally, the investment came in the form of users meticulously tracking their fitness journey within the app.

This ingenious design created a self-perpetuating loop. The more users shared their workout routines, the more social validation they received, encouraging them to invest further in the app and continue the cycle. It was a testament to the power of understanding the psychology of users and building products that cater not only to their needs but also to their innate desires for connection and recognition.

Remember, engagement triumphs over mere broadcasting. Create dialogues instead of spreading news. Seek feedback; involve your users in the decisions that shape your product. True marketing does not feel like marketing. A thriving community, a collective of believers, will sell for you, defend your brand against all detractors, and ensure unwavering customer loyalty.

Sridhar once had the opportunity to collaborate with a dynamic startup that was developing an innovative online game. From the outset, they embraced the principles of the lean startup method, recognizing the importance of iterative development and continuous feedback. They implemented a 'build-measure-learn' feedback loop, creating a vibrant online forum where users could actively participate in the evolution of the game.

The founders were deeply engaged in this community, eagerly soliciting suggestions, responding to criticism, and rapidly incorporating user feedback into their development process. This created a remarkable synergy between the creators and the players, fostering a sense of shared ownership and a loyal community that was genuinely invested in the game's success.

The results were striking. The game evolved at an impressive pace, bringing it closer to the desires and expectations of the target audience with each iteration. Features that resonated with players were amplified, while those that proved less popular were refined or discarded. This constant feedback loop ensured that the final product was not just a game created by the developers but a collaborative effort—a testament to the power of listening to your users.

This experience served as a powerful reminder that successful products are not created in a vacuum. They are shaped by the needs and desires of the people who will ultimately use them. By embracing the lean startup methodology and fostering a culture of open communication and collaboration, this startup was able to create a game that truly resonated with players, building a thriving community in the process.

The Formula for Selling Your Vision

Persuasion, my friend, is the weapon that wins over your initial followers. If you cannot sell, you cannot grow. Your first hundred users are the cornerstones of your future. Secure them, and they will multiply your reach exponentially. Digital growth is not an option; it is a necessity. SEO, social media and strategic advertising must work together in a harmonious concert. Branding and storytelling are your most potent weapons. Imbue your customers with a belief in your mission, with conviction about your purpose. Remember that community equals sustainable growth. If your creation ignites passion in the hearts of others, they will spread the word with fervour. Let this be etched into your mind: Sales is not a department; it is the lifeblood of your entire business.

Up Next: From Selling a Vision to Building a Visionary Team

You have mastered the art of selling your vision, acquiring your first customers, and building momentum through the power of digital growth. But let's face the unvarnished truth: No startup can achieve true scale without the right people who share your fire. Your product will not materialize by mere wishful thinking. Your customers will not stay engaged without the driving force of innovation. Your startup's success is a direct reflection of the team you assemble, the collective of minds and hands that will bring your vision to life.

Building a company that will alter the course of history begins with the creation of a team that is equally transformative. Your greatest challenge, beyond product development or fundraising, is assembling the right people together and ensuring they are aligned with your vision.

Let's Build a Rockstar Team

Let us now embark on the journey of building a team of exceptional individuals, a team that will not merely execute tasks but also ignite a revolution.

4

People Power: Crafting Culture and Leadership

A magnificent idea, a vision of untold wealth, a concept that could reshape industries—all these are but empty vessels without the right hands to steer them. Here is a vital truth: A great idea, bereft of the right people, is utterly worthless. For in the grand tapestry of success, it is not the brilliance of the concept alone that weaves the golden thread, but the collective might of those who bring it to fruition.

Let us dispel the illusions plaguing the minds of those seeking prosperity. Startups, those fledgling enterprises that promise vast fortunes, do not crumble due to a dearth of funding or a lack of a brilliant product. No, the true culprit is the absence of a team capable of execution at the highest level. The seeds of failure are sown when the foundation of the venture is built upon individuals who lack the unwavering determination and unified purpose necessary to transform vision into reality.

Execution: The Keystone of Achievement

Execution, this vital force that breathes life into dreams, is the essence of success. And execution, I tell you, is a direct function of the individuals you enlist, the manner in which you lead them, and the culture you cultivate within your ranks. Remember a leader without a capable team is a general without an army, a conductor without an orchestra. It is the harmonious synergy of talent, dedication and shared purpose that propels a venture toward its ultimate destiny.

The Myth of the Solitary Founder

No founder, no matter how visionary, achieves monumental success in isolation. The difference between a startup that ascends to the heights of a billion-dollar enterprise and one that descends into the abyss of failure within its nascent years is, without exception, the team that stands behind it. It is the collective energy, unified resolve and unwavering commitment of the team that transforms a mere idea into a thriving empire.

The Testament of Giants: Airbnb, Paytm, Razorpay, Zoho

Consider the titans of industry, the giants that have reshaped the landscape of commerce: Airbnb, Paytm, Razorpay and Zoho. These monumental enterprises did not rise to dominance through the strength of a single visionary founder alone. No, they achieved their greatness by assembling teams that shared a singular obsession and worked relentlessly towards a common goal. It is the power of collective purpose, the unwavering commitment of a unified team that forges the path to enduring success.

Let's delve into the nature of their triumphs, strip away the veneer of chance, and reveal the bedrock of their success. Take Airbnb, for example. The company's meteoric rise was not based on a novel idea alone but on the meticulous cultivation of a team that embodied the spirit of hospitality and innovation. They empowered their hosts, fostered a community, and built a platform where every member felt a sense of belonging—a testament to the power of unified purpose.

Similarly, Paytm's rise to dominance was fuelled by a team that relentlessly pursued the vision of seamless digital transactions, overcoming formidable obstacles with unwavering determination. They forged a culture of rapid iteration and customer-centricity, proving that collective resolve can conquer even the most challenging markets. Razorpay, in its relentless pursuit of revolutionizing online payments, assembled a team of engineers and innovators who shared an unyielding commitment to excellence. They fostered an environment where problem-solving was paramount and innovation was ingrained in their DNA.

Zoho, a testament to the power of organic growth, built a team that embodied the values of craftsmanship and long-term vision. They nurtured talent from within, fostering a culture of continuous learning and unwavering dedication, proving that true success is built on a foundation of shared values and sustained effort. These are not mere anecdotes but irrefutable evidence that the alchemy of a powerful team united in purpose and driven by unwavering commitment is the true catalyst for extraordinary achievement.

Therefore, seek not merely brilliant ideas but cultivate the power of the right people, for therein lies the true secret to amassing a fortune.

4.1 THE DNA OF A HIGH-PERFORMING TEAM

Your initial selections, those first souls you bring aboard, they are not mere employees; they are the very architects of your company's destiny. Understand this: A fledgling enterprise is not a polished, predictable machine. It is a battlefield, a crucible where the mettle of men and women is tested. Those early recruits, they are your vanguard, your first line of defence. They shape not merely the tangible product but the very essence of your enterprise—its culture, its velocity, its enduring strength. To err in these early selections, to bring in those ill-suited to the fight, is to court certain demise. Your venture will wither before it has a chance to blossom.

Most businesses, trapped in conventional thinking, believe hiring is merely a matter of filling vacant roles. They are tragically mistaken. In the realm of the startup, hiring is an act of summoning forth problem-solvers, individuals who do not wait for commands but forge their own path.

> Shreeram recalls working with a founder who was deeply passionate about his startup's mission, yet he was struggling to build a team that shared his enthusiasm. He had hired talented individuals, but they seemed more interested in fulfilling their job descriptions than contributing to the company's overarching vision. He confided that he felt like he was carrying the weight of the world on his shoulders, and he was exhausted.
>
> Shreeram introduced him to the 'who method',[20] a hiring framework that emphasises the importance of defining clear expectations and conducting structured interviews.

> The Who Method is a structured hiring framework developed by Geoff Smart and Randy Street that focuses on defining clear expectations through scorecards, sourcing top talent, conducting structured interviews, and selecting candidates based on objective grading to build a team of A-players.
>
> Together, we crafted a scorecard that prioritized not only technical skills but also passion for the problem the startup was addressing, alignment with the company's mission, and key competencies such as resilience, adaptability and a collaborative spirit.
>
> Armed with this new approach, he began to seek out candidates who weren't simply looking for a job; he sought individuals who were genuinely inspired by the startup's vision and eager to contribute to its success. The results were transformative. He assembled a team of dedicated individuals who were not only skilled but also deeply invested in the company's mission. This shift in hiring strategy not only improved employee morale and productivity but also freed the founder to focus on his strengths—leading, strategizing and driving the company forward.

These are the pioneers who thrive amidst uncertainty, who adapt to the chaos that is the lifeblood of a new venture, and who seize ownership when adversity strikes. Reflect upon the tales of legendary startups—Flipkart, Razorpay, Zerodha, Stripe and OpenAI. Their triumphs were not solely the product of visionary founders. They were built upon the bedrock of the first ten individuals, those who possessed the right spirit, the right drive, and the right mental fortitude.

The Traits of a High-Performing Startup Team

What distinguishes a startup team from its corporate counterpart? Let us examine the defining characteristics.

Obsession over compensation

Those who join a nascent enterprise should not be lured by mere trinkets and baubles. They must be driven by a profound obsession with the problem your startup seeks to solve. If the first words uttered by a candidate concern stock options or vacation policies, know that they are fundamentally misaligned. Consider Ritesh Agarwal, who in the early days of OYO lacked vast financial resources. His initial team laboured under severe budgetary constraints, fuelled by a shared belief in the vision of creating India's premier hospitality brand.

Bias for action

The startup environment is a race against time. There is no room for those paralysed by overthinking. Endless meetings, perfect conditions, or absolute clarity are luxuries a startup cannot afford. Decisive and swift action trumps theoretical musings every time. The founders of Zepto, for example, demonstrated this principle by outpacing their competitors. They did not wait for a flawless system; they iterated as they progressed, launching in record time.

Versatility is non-negotiable

In the fluid and ambiguous world of startups, roles are not rigidly defined. Your chief technology officer may find themselves answering customer service enquiries, and your designer may close pivotal deals. You require individuals who thrive in this environment of constant flux. Paytm's early team exemplified this—working across all domains, be it engineering, marketing or customer service. This adaptability was the catalyst for their rapid expansion.

Resilience through uncertainty

The path of a startup is fraught with peril. Setbacks are inevitable. Funding may evaporate, growth may falter, and plans may unravel. A high-performing team does not succumb to panic; they adapt, they persevere. The founders of Razorpay, for example, faced rejection from over a hundred investors. Yet, their unwavering belief in their product, fortified by the resilience of their team, propelled them to unicorn status.

> Shreeram vividly recalls working with a fledgling startup that was developing a new social media platform. The founders, brimming with passion and ambition, were fixated on achieving perfection before unveiling their creation to the world. They believed that a flawless product would guarantee instant success. However, Shreeram recognized the inherent danger in this approach—the risk of endlessly delaying the launch while the market evolved and competitors emerged.
>
> Drawing upon his experience, Shreeram gently steered them towards the principles of agile development,[21] an iterative approach that prioritizes flexibility and responsiveness. He encouraged them to release a functional version of their platform, a minimum viable product, and then continuously refine it based on user feedback and market dynamics.

> Agile software development is an iterative and flexible methodology that emphasises collaboration, continuous improvement, and rapid delivery of working software to adapt to changing customer needs and market demands.
>
> This shift in mindset proved transformative. By embracing an agile approach, the founders were able to quickly gather user insights, adapt their features, and address real-world needs. They transformed their initial offering into a dynamic, user-centred platform that resonated with their target audience. As a result, they gained traction and built a loyal user base far more rapidly than they had initially anticipated.
>
> This experience reinforced a fundamental truth of entrepreneurship: Perfection is an elusive goal, and the pursuit of it can often be a recipe for stagnation. In the dynamic world of startups, speed and adaptability are paramount. By embracing an iterative approach, founders can effectively navigate the uncertainties of the market, respond to user feedback, and ultimately increase their chances of success.

The Cost of Hiring the Wrong People

A misstep in hiring is far more detrimental than a vacant position. A flawed employee impedes progress, erodes morale and introduces bureaucratic inertia. Many startups perish not from flawed concepts but from the recruitment of individuals ill-suited to the startup ethos. The most perilous error is to hire those adept at maintaining existing systems but incapable of building from the ground up.

Your initial hires will form the cornerstone of your company's success. Seek those who are relentless problem-solvers, who embrace speed and execute with unwavering resolve. That, my friends, is the DNA of a high-performing startup team.

4.2 HIRING SLOW, FIRING FAST

A bad hire, my friends, is a far greater liability than an empty chair. In the arena of entrepreneurial conquest, every founder faces a critical decision: rush in and fill a void, or exercise patience and await the arrival of the truly worthy. Let's be clear: The expense of a misaligned individual far outweighs the temporary inconvenience of a vacant position. In the crucible of a startup, each soul bears immense significance. A flawed selection not only impedes progress, it poisons the culture, stifles momentum, and squanders precious resources. The most astute leaders who understand the true nature of success are dedicated to the art of hiring, knowing that a single errant choice can derail the entire enterprise.

Why Hiring Fast Can Kill a Startup

The illusion of speed in hiring often seduces those scaling their ventures; this is a perilous path. The cost of a hasty hire goes far beyond just salary; it consumes time, drains energy, and squanders invaluable opportunities. A hasty hire is akin to startup suicide. Understand this: culture-fit transcends mere skill. A single toxic presence can contaminate the entire spirit of your organization. Talent alone is not enough; if an individual breeds discord, hinders execution or saps morale, they become a liability. Remember, skills can be honed, but character is immutable. You can impart knowledge of coding or marketing, but you cannot instill the drive to take ownership, adaptability to uncertainty, or a genuine passion for your mission. Every employee represents an investment. Each must contribute to the growth of your enterprise. Those who fail to add value become a drain on the resources that sustain your vision.

> Sridhar vividly recalls a time when he was advising a burgeoning startup that was experiencing rapid growth. The company was facing immense pressure to fill a multitude of open positions, and the temptation to prioritize speed over diligence in their hiring process was palpable. However, Sridhar cautioned them against succumbing to this pressure, emphasising the importance of patience, thoroughness, and a commitment to finding the right individuals.
>
> To their credit, they heeded Sridhar's advice. They slowed down their hiring process, implemented more rigorous screening procedures, and invested the time necessary to truly understand the needs of each role and the qualifications of each candidate. As a result, they successfully navigated the potential minefield of bad hires, avoiding costly mistakes that could have hindered their growth trajectory and derailed their entire venture. This experience served as a powerful reminder that in the realm of startups, patience and discernment in hiring are not merely virtues; they are essential ingredients for sustainable success.

Why Firing Fast Is a Survival Strategy

Many founders falter when faced with the necessity of dismissal, succumbing to discomfort. But the longer you harbour a misfit, the greater the damage inflicted. Understand that dead weight slows down the entire team. Those who cannot perform not only hinder their own output but also burden their colleagues with the task of compensation. A small, elite team of A-players will always triumph over a large, mediocre assembly. Startups thrive on agility, on moving faster than their competitors. You don't just need numbers; you need the right individuals. If you find yourself crafting excuses to justify an individual's presence, then their departure is long overdue. This isn't about cruelty; it's about safeguarding the vitality of your company.

How to Hire Right and Fire Fast

Hiring is the cornerstone of your enterprise. It determines the speed of your ascent, the strength of your execution, and ultimately your survival. Yet many treat this critical process as a mere checklist, filtering candidates based on superficial credentials. This is a grave mistake. The biggest advantage of your startup is its speed. Your initial hires must be able to act quickly, thrive in chaos, and solve problems autonomously. A lengthy resume is meaningless without the ability to execute at startup velocity. And when an individual proves incompatible? Hesitation is your enemy. Firing, though unpleasant, is essential. Startups do not perish from a lack of funding or ideas; they perish from flawed execution, which stems from misaligned hires and prolonged retention.

Test for Hunger, Not Just Experience

The most common error in hiring is the overvaluation of experience and the undervaluation of hunger. A decade of resume entries is meaningless without adaptability, urgency and independent thought. Startups are forged by those who seize initiative, not those who await instruction. When hiring, ask yourself: Are they driven by a passion for problem-solving? Can they navigate ambiguity? Do they embrace ownership? Test their hunger by presenting real-world challenges, observing their curiosity, and gauging their energy. A startup seeks not the most experienced but the most driven.

Set Expectations Early

Securing the right talent is merely the first step. You must also ensure they comprehend the expectations from their first day. Startups cannot afford prolonged onboarding or gradual acclimation. Clarity is paramount. Define clear milestones for the first 30, 60 and 90 days. Assign meaningful projects from the outset. Be brutally honest about the demands of your startup.

Fire without Guilt

Dismissal is the most challenging aspect of leadership. Yet, hesitation is a fatal flaw. Every day wasted on the wrong individual is a day lost for your enterprise. If an individual is slow, disruptive, or unproductive, they jeopardize the entire team. If you find yourself making excuses, you already know the answer. Look for these signs: constant handholding, missed deadlines, energy depletion and mere adequacy. Firing is not personal; it is protective.

The Best Startups Aren't Afraid to Fire

The most successful companies embrace swift dismissal, understanding that a single misaligned individual can impede the progress of the entire team. They know that a month wasted on the wrong hire is a month lost for the business.

What Founders Get Wrong about Hiring

They rush the process, they prolong the retention of misfits, and they fail to prioritize recruitment.

How to Hire Right and Fire Fast

Seek hunger over experience, set clear expectations, dismiss without guilt, and never tolerate mediocrity. Hiring is not merely team building; it is the construction of a winning machine. The right hires will propel your company forward. The wrong hires will destroy it. Be ruthless. Hire slowly and fire swiftly. Your company's fate depends on it.

> Sridhar once worked with a founder who was grappling with the difficult decision of letting go of an underperforming employee. He knew it needed to be done, but he hesitated, worried about the impact on morale and the potential disruption to the team. Sridhar introduced him to the 'hire slow, fire fast' principle, explaining that sometimes swift action is necessary to protect the overall health and productivity of the team.
>
> The principle of 'hire slow, fire fast'[22] emphasises taking time to carefully vet candidates during hiring to ensure alignment with company values and goals, while swiftly

> letting go of underperforming employees to minimize organizational damage.
>
> He took the advice to heart, and once the decision was made, Sridhar saw an immediate shift. The team dynamic improved, their focus sharpened, and ultimately, their performance exceeded expectations. It reinforced the importance of making those tough calls when necessary, not just for the company's well-being but for the team's as well.

4.3 CREATING A CULTURE OF ACCOUNTABILITY AND INNOVATION

Let us be clear that the mere trappings of a modern office, the illusion of freedom afforded by flexible working hours, or the superficial camaraderie of casual Fridays are but fleeting distractions. The true culture, the bedrock upon which empires of success are built, lies at the very marrow of your organization. It is revealed in the crucible of decision-making, in the swift and decisive resolution of challenges, and in the unwavering cohesion of your teams when the pressure mounts. It is most vividly displayed when the world threatens to crumble, when deadlines loom like a hangman's noose, and when your venture teeters on the precipice of oblivion. The titans of the industry—Razorpay, CRED, Stripe and OpenAI—are each a testament to a culture that champions accountability, ownership and an unyielding pursuit of innovation. Without this vital essence, a company is destined to wither in the barren landscape of mediocrity or be strangled by the suffocating grip of bureaucratic paralysis before it can ever achieve the scale it aspires to.

How to Build a Culture of Accountability

Accountability is neither the heavy hand of micromanagement nor the petty tyranny of incessant oversight. Rather, it is the setting of an unassailable standard, the unwavering demand for results, and the cultivation of collective ownership where each individual feels the weight of his or her contribution. A startup, in its nascent stages, cannot afford the luxury of passengers—every soul must be a driver, steering the ship towards its destined harbour.

1. Make everyone an owner

Your earliest team members must think and act like founders. To merely work for a pay cheque is to diminish the soul of your company. The most successful startups don't just hire employees; they cultivate owners—people who are deeply invested in the company's mission, growth and long-term success.

Look at Tesla in its early days. Elon Musk didn't just build a car company—he built a movement, where the first employees weren't just engineers and marketers but pioneers on a mission to revolutionize transportation. Employees were granted equity, autonomy and a shared responsibility for the future of Tesla. This ownership mentality was what allowed Tesla to push through manufacturing crises, production delays and financial hurdles, to become a dominant force in the electric vehicles industry.

Empower your people with more than just a salary—give them a stake in the outcome. Involve them in strategic decisions, hold them accountable for growth, and watch them build with the same tenacity and vision as a founder.

Sridhar vividly recalls working with a fledgling startup that was grappling with the pervasive challenge of employee demotivation. The atmosphere in the company was palpably lacklustre, with disengaged employees merely going through the motions, their productivity stagnating. It was evident that a profound shift was needed to reignite the team's passion and unlock their true potential.

Drawing upon my understanding of self-determination theory (SDT)[23] is a psychological framework that explains human motivation based on the fulfilment of three innate needs: autonomy, competence and relatedness, driving self-motivated and self-determined behaviours.

Sridhar embarked on a mission to cultivate an environment that nurtured the three fundamental psychological needs: autonomy, competence and relatedness. He initiated this transformation by granting employees greater autonomy, empowering them to make decisions and contribute their unique perspectives. This newfound sense of ownership instilled a renewed sense of purpose and ignited their intrinsic motivation.

To foster competence, Sridhar implemented a comprehensive programme that provided employees with opportunities to enhance their skills and expand their knowledge base. Through workshops, mentorship initiatives and challenging assignments, they were able to develop their capabilities and experience a sense of mastery in their respective roles.

Recognizing the profound impact of social connections on motivation, Sridhar prioritized fostering a sense of relatedness within the team. He encouraged collaboration,

> created opportunities for team bonding, and cultivated an inclusive environment where everyone felt valued and supported. This emphasis on camaraderie and belonging strengthened relationships and created a sense of shared purpose.
>
> The results of this multifaceted approach were nothing short of remarkable. As employees felt increasingly empowered, capable and connected, their motivation soared. They approached their work with renewed enthusiasm, their productivity surged, and the once-stagnant atmosphere was replaced by a vibrant energy that permeated the entire organization.

2. Results over hours worked

Mere toil is not a measure of worth; results are the gold standard. A culture of accountability does not glorify the empty ritual of long hours or the hollow mantra of hustle. It rewards those who deliver, who transform vision into tangible reality. An example of this is the founders of Zerodha, who built a culture where innovation and execution trumped the mere expenditure of time. They disrupted the Indian brokerage market by focusing on efficiency, not simply effort. Set clear, measurable goals, judging by impact, not effort. Eradicate the insidious 'hours worked' mentality.

Reward outcomes, not the mere passage of time. If a person incessantly proclaims their 'hard work' yet produces nothing of substance, they are a misfit, a hindrance to your grand design.

Shreeram once worked with a startup that had fallen into the trap of equating long hours with productivity. Their incentive system inadvertently rewarded employees for presenteeism rather than results. This led to a culture where people felt pressured to stay late, regardless of whether they were actually accomplishing anything meaningful. Burnout was high, and morale was low.

He saw an opportunity to apply a concept known as nudge theory,[24] which suggests that subtle changes in the environment can influence people's choices and behaviour.

Nudge theory is a behavioural science concept that proposes people's decisions and behaviours can be influenced in predictable ways by subtle changes in how choices are presented to them, without restricting freedom of choice or changing economic incentives.

Instead of completely overhauling their system, Shreeram focused on redesigning their incentives. The company shifted the emphasis from effort to outcomes, rewarding employees for achieving specific goals and key performance indicators.

This seemingly small change had a profound impact. Employees began to prioritize efficiency and focus on tasks that truly moved the needle. They felt empowered to manage their time effectively and were no longer incentivized to simply 'look busy'. The result was a significant improvement in the overall company performance, accompanied by a noticeable boost in employee satisfaction and engagement. It was a powerful reminder that sometimes the most effective solutions are not the most complex ones but the ones that gently nudge people in the right direction.

3. Transparency drives trust

Most enterprises treat their people as mere cogs, obediently following instructions. The truly great treat them as partners, sharing the sacred knowledge of finances, strategy and the inevitable challenges that arise. Tony Xu, in building DoorDash, a food delivery and ordering service that connects customers with restaurants and drivers, shared both triumphs and setbacks, fostering a team that embraced ownership rather than retreating from adversity. Share your financials, challenges and strategies openly. Allow your people to grapple with the problems to contribute to their resolution. Build trust through absolute transparency. Those kept in the dark will act as mere employees, not as the owners you require.

4. No room for mediocrity

A culture of excellence is not born from comfort; it is forged in the crucible of high expectations and relentless progress. True greatness demands an environment where each individual drives the other to push boundaries, where stagnation is unacceptable, and where ambition is the shared language. To tolerate mediocrity is to resign your company to mediocrity.

Take Reed Hastings at Netflix. From the very beginning, he cultivated a culture of high performance, famously stating, 'adequate performance gets a generous severance.' He sought not just skilled professionals but those who thrived under responsibility, who could make bold decisions, and who saw the company's success as their own. The result? Netflix disrupted and dominated the entertainment industry, not just through innovation but through a workforce built on intellectual rigour, accountability and uncompromising standards.

Set the bar unapologetically high. Surround yourself with those who challenge and elevate each other. Deliver feedback without hesitation—sharp, precise and constructive. Move swiftly in correcting inefficiencies, and if necessary, remove those who hinder progress. A single wrong hire doesn't just slow down execution; it poisons momentum. If you want to build something legendary, ensure that your culture demands it.

How to Foster Innovation

Innovation is not the exclusive domain of a 'creative team'. It is the product of an environment where ideas are tested, executed and refined with relentless speed. A startup that fails to innovate is a startup that is destined to perish.

1. Encourage smart risks

If your team fears risk, your company will remain stuck in mediocrity. The greatest companies do not punish failure; they punish the reluctance to try.

Consider Tobi Lütke, the founder of Shopify. Instead of following conventional e-commerce models, he took a bold risk—building a platform that allowed anyone to create an online store without technical expertise. Many doubted that small businesses would adopt it, but that risk transformed Shopify into the backbone of global e-commerce.

Foster a culture where experimentation is encouraged. Reward initiative, even when it leads to failure, because every failure is a lesson that accelerates innovation. Build an environment where people are empowered to take bold bets, knowing that true breakthroughs come not from playing it safe but from pushing boundaries.

2. Eliminate bureaucracy

If the process becomes a shackle, slowing the pace of decision-making, your startup is already in its death throes. The most astute founders dismantle red tape, allowing ideas to materialize from concept to execution in days, not months. Stripe, in its inception, ensured seamless developer integration, mirroring an internal culture that swiftly tested and launched ideas. Reduce approvals and eliminate superfluous meetings. Create a culture of relentless execution. If an idea holds promise, test it immediately. If bureaucracy impedes progress, excise it without mercy.

3. Hire people smarter than you

The most successful founders are not the ones who know everything—they are the ones who build a team of experts smarter than themselves. If you are the sharpest mind in your company, your business is destined to plateau.

Consider Patu Keswani, the founder of Lemon Tree, an Indian hotel chain that operates a variety of hotels, including upscale, midscale and economy hotels. He didn't build one of India's leading hospitality chains by trying to run every department himself. Instead, he brought in top-tier professionals in hotel management, operations and customer experience, empowering them to execute with precision while he focused on vision and strategy.

Prioritize intelligence over titles. Surround yourself with those who challenge your assumptions and elevate your thinking. If you consistently find yourself the most knowledgeable person in the room, it's a sign you need to hire better.

The Culture That Wins

A startup's destiny is not solely determined by its product but by the execution, ownership and innovation of its team. Accountability demands drivers, not passengers, to take ownership at every level and results in mere effort. Innovation requires the courage to take smart risks, the eradication of bureaucratic shackles, and the humility to surround yourself with superior minds. The startups that ascend to greatness are built upon cultures that demand the best. If you cultivate the right culture, innovation and accountability will flourish organically, becoming the very essence of your company's operation.

4.4 MANAGING CO-FOUNDER AND EMPLOYEE CONFLICTS

Let it be known, my friends, that conflict in any enterprise, especially in the tempestuous realm of a startup, is not a mere possibility; it is an absolute certainty. In the crucible of building something new, tensions will inevitably arise, like storms on a turbulent sea. Co-founders, those who embark on this journey together, will find themselves at odds, their visions clashing. Employees, the very lifeblood of the venture, may feel undervalued, their contributions overlooked. Understand this: The true measure of a startup's potential lies not in the absence of conflict but in the ability to manage and resolve it before it festers and poisons the entire enterprise.

Why Co-Founder Conflicts Destroy Startups

Examine the wreckage of failed startups, and a stark truth will emerge—more ventures perish from internal strife than from the fiercest market competition. Consider the titans of industry today—Facebook, Flipkart and Snapdeal. Behind the veneer of success, nearly every major startup has endured founder battles, leadership disputes and power struggles. Mark Zuckerberg's clash with Eduardo Saverin, a tempest of legal wrangling over equity and ownership, nearly capsized Facebook.[25] The battle between Flipkart's[26] Sachin and Binny Bansal reshaped the leadership of a colossus. Snapdeal's[27] founders engaged in a public rift that threatened to dismantle the company entirely. When co-founder relationships sour, they do not merely fracture friendships; they extinguish the very life force of the company.

> Sridhar once had the opportunity to mentor a founder who was navigating a particularly challenging period of co-founder conflict. The tension between them had escalated to a point where it threatened to derail the entire venture. Recognizing the urgency of the situation, Sridhar introduced them to the interest-based relational approach[28] (IBRA), a powerful framework for conflict resolution that emphasises shared interests and collaborative problem-solving.
>
> The interest-based relational approach is a conflict resolution strategy that prioritizes building and maintaining relationships while addressing the underlying interests of all parties involved, achieving mutually beneficial outcomes through collaboration and understanding.
>
> Initially, their interactions were characterized by positional arguments—each founder entrenched in their own perspective, unwilling to concede ground. Through IBRA, Sridhar encouraged them to shift their focus from rigid stances to a deeper understanding of each other's underlying needs and motivations. This involved

> fostering active listening, creating a safe space for open communication, and guiding them towards a collaborative approach to problem-solving.
>
> The transformation was remarkable. As they began to truly listen to each other, to understand the 'why' behind their respective positions, a sense of empathy emerged. They started to see the situation not as a battle to be won but as a shared challenge to be overcome. They identified common goals, rebuilt trust, and ultimately emerged from the conflict as a stronger, more unified team. The experience served as a powerful reminder that even in the most challenging of circumstances, the principles of collaboration and understanding can pave the way for growth and success.

How to Prevent Co-founder Conflicts before They Start

The wisest course is to prevent conflicts before they ignite. Most co-founder disputes stem from murky expectations, undefined roles and the clash of egos. Therefore, define roles from the very outset.

When co-founders tread on each other's domains, conflict is inevitable. Who will oversee product, growth, hiring and fundraising? Who will make the final decision in times of disagreement? How will responsibilities evolve as the company expands? If these questions remain unanswered, resentment will fester. Align yourselves not just on execution but on the very vision of the enterprise. Do you seek to build a billion-dollar empire or a profitable, sustainable venture? Are you prepared for a swift exit, or do you envision a long-term legacy?

Will you prioritize profitability or relentless growth? Are you willing to pivot, or will you remain steadfast to the original concept? Without this alignment, even the smallest decisions become battlegrounds. And, most importantly, commit everything to writing before it is needed. Many founders, in their early enthusiasm, neglect legal agreements, trusting solely in their bond. But trust alone will not prevent legal disputes when fortunes are at stake. Document equity splits, decision-making power and exit terms. A written agreement is not a sign of distrust but a safeguard against misunderstandings that could shatter everything you have built.

> In the fast-paced world of startups, where innovation and agility reign supreme, conflict among team members can be a significant impediment to progress. Shreeram vividly recalls a particular startup he consulted with, where a diverse group of individuals, each brimming with ideas and driven by a shared passion for their venture, found themselves entangled in a web of disagreements and misunderstandings.
>
> The team was composed of a seasoned CEO with a penchant for micromanagement, a CTO who fiercely guarded his domain, a marketing manager eager to make her mark, and a handful of brilliant yet somewhat territorial engineers. Their conflicting perspectives on project ownership and decision-making authority created a breeding ground for friction, hindering their ability to collaborate effectively and impeding their overall productivity.
>
> Recognizing the urgent need for clarity and structure, we introduced the team to the RACI[29] matrix, a powerful tool for defining roles and responsibilities with precision.

RACI is a project management framework that clarifies roles and responsibilities by categorizing team members as Responsible (does the work), Accountable (ensures task completion), Consulted (provides input), or Informed (kept in the loop).

We meticulously mapped out each task and decision involved in their product development process, assigning clear ownership levels:

- **Responsible:** The individual or team responsible for executing the task.
- **Accountable:** The person ultimately answerable for the outcome of the task.
- **Consulted:** Those whose input is sought before a decision is made or a task is executed.
- **Informed:** Those who need to be kept in the loop regarding the progress of a task or decision.

As we worked through the matrix, a sense of order began to emerge from the chaos. The CEO, accustomed to being involved in every detail, learned to delegate effectively and trust his team's expertise. The CTO, reassured that his authority over technical matters was clearly defined, became more receptive to input from others. The marketing manager, empowered with a clear understanding of her role in the product development process, was able to channel her enthusiasm into strategic initiatives that aligned with the company's overall vision. And the engineers, relieved of the burden of constantly defending their turf, were able to focus their energy on what they did best: building innovative products.

> The RACI matrix served as a catalyst for transformation, fostering a culture of collaboration and mutual respect. By eliminating ambiguity and clarifying expectations, it enabled the team to work together seamlessly, leveraging their diverse strengths to achieve common goals. The result was a dramatic improvement in productivity, a renewed sense of purpose, and a shared commitment to the company's success.

How to Handle Employee Conflicts before They Get Toxic

It is not only co-founders who clash; employee conflicts can cripple morale, hinder progress, and breed a culture of toxicity. A startup can withstand marketing missteps, hiring errors and even flawed products, but it cannot survive a toxic culture. If employees turn against each other, the venture is doomed. Resolve conflicts swiftly, before they spread. Most conflicts do not erupt overnight; they simmer beneath the surface. If an employee feels undervalued, they may not speak up, but they will disengage. If another feels their work is unappreciated, they may seek opportunities elsewhere. Address tensions immediately; minor issues ignored become insurmountable problems. Promote meritocracy, not politics. Resentment festers when hard work is overlooked for favouritism. Your culture should reward results, not noise. And cultivate an open-feedback culture. If employees fear speaking up, problems will remain unsolved. Create safe channels for feedback, encourage honest dialogue, and lead with transparency.

Conflict Is Inevitable: How You Handle It Is the Difference

The greatest startups do not avoid conflict; they master its management. Facebook weathered its co-founder's departure. Flipkart navigated leadership transitions. Apple thrived after the tumultuous exit and return of Steve Jobs. Conflict itself is not destructive; unresolved conflict is. Founders who define roles, align visions, document agreements, and confront issues head-on build resilient companies. Those who ignore problems watch their startups crumble. Startups are built on people. If those people cannot work together, the business will not endure. Master conflict resolution, and you will build not just a startup but a team capable of weathering any storm.

4.5 LEADERSHIP LESSONS FROM STARTUP GIANTS

Indeed, the very cornerstone of any successful enterprise, particularly within the dynamic realm of startups, is not merely the brilliance of the product itself but the calibre of leadership that galvanizes the team. It is a grave error to become so consumed by the minutiae of product development, the pursuit of funding, or the intricacies of scaling that one neglects the imperative of masterful leadership. No matter how ingenious the conception or how revolutionary the idea, a startup bereft of strong leadership is destined to falter and collapse. A startup, you see, is only as robust as the individuals who constitute it, and these individuals, these vital components, do not blindly follow abstract notions; they follow leaders. It is the quality of leadership, not mere charisma or the inflated ego, that distinguishes those startups that flourish from those that implode. It is the ability to forge, to inspire, to empower a team capable of delivering under the relentless pressure of the entrepreneurial journey.

Learn from the Best: Leadership in Action

Throughout the annals of business, it is evident that the most exceptional startup leaders share fundamental principles. They do not merely employ individuals; they cultivate cultures. They do not merely manage subordinates; they forge high-performance teams. Consider, for instance, the masters who have achieved this:

1. Reed Hastings, Netflix—culture over comfort

Netflix, that global entertainment powerhouse, did not ascend to its lofty position by mere chance. Reed Hastings, with unwavering resolve, instituted a leadership culture where only the most exceptional could thrive. His philosophy, succinctly put, was a rejection of 'brilliant jerks'. Netflix is renowned for its stringent hiring standards and its uncompromising transparency. While it compensates generously, it swiftly parts ways with those who underperform. Hastings brooks no mediocrity, understanding that a single extraordinary employee far surpasses ten ordinary ones. Within Netflix, employees are granted full autonomy, yet they are held accountable for their decisions. Political manoeuvring is anathema; only performance matters. Job security is nonexistent, with all expected to deliver exceptional results or depart. If you aspire to lead as Hastings did, you must construct a performance-driven culture. Seek out those who are self-reliant and thrive on ownership. Do not provide a safety net for mediocrity.

2. Narayana Murthy, Infosys—founder's frugality and ethical leadership

Narayana Murthy built Infosys (a global IT services and consulting company that provides digital services to businesses) from humble beginnings with unwavering discipline and a long-term vision, not by squandering vast sums of capital but by adhering to the principles of frugality and ethical conduct. His maxim, 'When in doubt, disclose,' became the bedrock of Infosys's reputation as one of India's most respected IT giants. Murthy's leadership principles are clear: founders should take the least and give the most, prioritizing the wellbeing of their employees. A long-term perspective is essential, eschewing fleeting profits in favour of sustainable growth. Ethical leadership is paramount, as trust is the foundation upon which any successful team is built. Too many startup founders squander resources and overhype growth. Murthy took the opposite path, building Infosys as a marathon, not a sprint. His model is worth emulating for anyone who wants to build lasting enterprises.

3. Ritesh Agarwal, OYO—scale requires people, not just strategy

OYO's rapid expansion from a single budget hotel to a global hospitality giant was not merely a matter of strategic expansion but a testament to the power of hiring problem-solvers. Agarwal understood that true scaling was impossible without a team capable of navigating the chaos. In fast-growing startups, perfect plans are an illusion. Teams must be adept at real-time problem-solving. Individuals who await instructions impede progress; hire those who can think independently. Scaling is not just about numbers; it is also about speed of execution.

OYO's rapid expansion was made possible by a team capable of operating without micromanagement.

Many founders mistakenly believe that systems and strategies alone drive growth. At OYO, it was the people. A strategy is inconsequential without a team built for speed, uncertainty and problem-solving.

The Three Critical Traits of Startup Leaders

Outstanding leadership transcends titles and authority; it is about inspiring others to perform. The most effective startup leaders possess three core traits:

1. **Build a high-trust, high-performance culture**: Employees who lack trust in their leadership will not give their best. Honesty, uncompromising standards and swift action on underperformance are essential. Hastings, Murthy and Agarwal built companies where performance reigns supreme.
2. **Create leaders, not followers:** True leaders do not micromanage but cultivate other leaders. They empower individuals to think independently and take ownership of their decisions.
3. **Make the hard decisions that no one else wants to make**: Leadership demands tough choices: hiring, firing, pivoting, shutting down and navigating investor deals. Hesitation is fatal. Great leaders act decisively.

Your Team Is Your Startup

The difference between a billion-dollar company and a failed startup is not just the product but the team that builds it.

Hire deliberately, act decisively against underperformance, foster a culture of accountability and innovation, resolve conflicts swiftly, and learn from the masters of leadership. Your product will not sell itself, your business model will not fix itself, and your startup will not scale without the right team. As a founder, it is your duty to build and lead that team.

Up Next: The Founder's Mindset—Resilience and Adaptability

A superior product cannot salvage a weak founder. A robust business model cannot shield a leader who succumbs to pressure. The distinction between startups that endure and those that collapse is not merely money, technology or timing, but also the founder's mindset. Entrepreneurship is a test of endurance. Those who prevail are not necessarily the most intelligent or connected; they are those who refuse to yield. Leading a team is one endeavor; leading oneself through uncertainty and high-stakes decisions is another. The subsequent chapter will delve into the psychological dimensions of entrepreneurship, exploring the development of resilience, adaptability and mental fortitude required to thrive.

5

The Founder's Mindset: Resilience and Adaptability

Let's be clear: building a startup is not simply the launch of a business; it is forging a mindset, a steely resolve capable of withstanding the relentless uncertainty that is the air entrepreneurs breathe. Understand this and understand it well: anything that can go wrong will go wrong. Funds will evaporate like morning mist, customers will desert you, markets will shift like sand in a storm, and competitors will materialize from thin air. So what distinguishes those who triumph from those who crumble? It's not just the intelligence, nor the funding, nor the connections—it is the unwavering resilience and lightning-fast adaptability that separate the victors from the vanquished.

This book lays out the tactical and strategic foundations for building a startup, from identifying real problems to the acquisition of capital, the conquest of customers, and the assembly of a world-class team. All of these are but tools in the hands of a craftsman; without the fortitude to endure, the flexibility to evolve, and the sheer grit to execute under the crushing weight of pressure, these tools are useless.

Every founder dreams of success, but few grasp the true cost of survival on the long, arduous road. The most formidable companies in the world did not emerge from a cradle of comfort; they were forged in the crucible of adversity. Those founders who ascended to greatness did not merely navigate chaos—they embraced it; they thrived within it. Survival, my friends, is the ultimate competitive advantage. This chapter, therefore, is not a discourse on mere business mechanics; it is a treatise on the psychology of winning, on the mental endurance, adaptability, and sheer force of will required to transform an idea into a lasting impact, to cultivate the founder's mindset—the very edge that distinguishes those who fade into obscurity from those who etch their names into the annals of history.

The Unspoken Reality of Entrepreneurship

Many founders embark on their entrepreneurial journey misled by fanciful myths, their minds filled with illusions. The media, in its relentless pursuit of sensationalism, glorifies billion-dollar valuations, flashy product launches and glamorous tech conferences, but rarely, if ever, illuminates the stark reality of sleepless nights, the cold sweat of payroll panic, the soul-crushing despair of relentless rejections, and the profound loneliness that comes with leadership. The reality is as unforgiving as it is stark: over 90 per cent of startups fail, the majority of first-time founders never achieve success, and even the most brilliant ideas can wither and die without relentless execution. The greatest misconception? That success hinges solely on having the best product.

It is execution, endurance and adaptability that reign supreme. Steve Jobs did not invent the personal computer; he mastered execution and vision. Elon Musk did not invent electric vehicles; he outlasted the sceptics and the setbacks. Falguni Nayar did not invent beauty e-commerce; she built Nykaa through relentless focus and unwavering determination. The founders who ascend to the heights of success think differently; they are not just business builders; they are warriors engaged in a high-stakes battle for survival.

Everything before This Was Just Preparation

To be unequivocal, the preceding chapters have laid the groundwork, the essential pillars on which startup success is built—identifying market gaps, mastering sales, securing funding and assembling high-performance teams. In Chapter 1, we learnt that solving a real problem is the foundation of a great startup; the best companies don't just launch products—they eliminate pain points with such surgical precision that customers cannot ignore them. In Chapter 2, we saw that startups do not fail due to bad ideas but due to catastrophic financial decisions.

Cash is the lifeblood of your enterprise; squander it, and you perish. Raise money without discipline, and you still perish. The founders who control their finances control their destiny. In Chapter 3, we uncovered the stark truth that a product never sells itself; the most successful startups do not merely market; they persuade, they sell, they capture mindshare with such ferocity that they dominate. We assure you that the first 100 customers are more challenging to acquire than the next million.

In Chapter 4, we focused on the most vital asset of all: people. Without the right team, execution collapses. The best founders are also the best recruiters, leaders and cultural architects; a dysfunctional team can sabotage even the most promising startup. None of this is enough. You can master every strategy, know your market inside and out, raise millions, craft the perfect pitch, and hire the most brilliant minds, but your startup will crumble if you lack the fortitude to withstand pressure, rejection and uncertainty.

The Mental Game: Why Founders Break

The startup world is a relentless, unforgiving arena. Most founders begin with a surge of excitement and optimism, but few endure the trials of the first few years. Why is that? They underestimate the time required for success. Overnight success stories are mere illusions and most great companies are built through years of relentless effort. They succumb to burnout; startups consume everything—your time, energy, relationships and mental health; many founders push themselves until they break. They fail to adapt quickly enough; markets shift, technology evolves, and what worked yesterday may be obsolete today. If you don't learn constantly, you die. Survival, therefore, is not merely about business strategy; it is about mental toughness. So the question is: can you outlast the struggle?

What the Best Founders Do Differently

1. **They expect chaos—and thrive in it:** A truly great founder not only accepts uncertainty but embraces it and makes it their weapon. Reed Hastings built Netflix by anticipating the demise of DVDs before anyone else. Ola's Bhavish Aggarwal pivoted with lightning speed when Uber entered India. Elon Musk made Tesla a survival-first company when it teetered on the brink of bankruptcy. If you expect a smooth journey, you are living in a fool's paradise.

2. **They treat failure as fuel:** Most people cower in fear of failure; founders embrace it. Kunal Shah built multiple failed products before discovering the path to success in fintech. Evan Spiegel launched numerous unsuccessful projects before founding Snapchat. Jack Ma was turned down for countless jobs before founding Alibaba. Failure, my friends, is data; it reveals what's not working, enabling you to change course.
3. **They pivot without ego:** Many founders stubbornly cling to their original course even when it can lead to ruin. Zomato began as a restaurant discovery platform before evolving into a food delivery service. Instagram was once a failed location-based social network before becoming a photo-sharing phenomenon. Slack began as an internal tool for a failed gaming startup.
4. **They invest in their mental toughness:** Startups test not only business models but also the mettle of their founders. They do not let emotions dictate their decisions; pressure amplifies bad choices. They protect their mental energy; burnout is the inevitable result of unchecked stress. They surround themselves with those who challenge them; success is never achieved in isolation.
5. **They play the long game:** Most startups perish because their founders give up prematurely. Falguni Nayar built Nykaa over a decade. Amazon operated at a loss for years before becoming an e-commerce giant. If you are not thinking in decades, you are not thinking big enough.

Survival Is the Greatest Strategy

This chapter is not a mere theoretical exercise; it is a distillation of what it truly takes to prevail. Everything that preceded this—

problem-solving, sales prowess, funding, and team—is rendered useless if you succumb to pressure. Entrepreneurship rewards those who refuse to surrender, not because surrender is not an option but because the greatest founders see failure not as an end point but as a chapter in their grand narrative. The next chapter is about resilience, adaptation and the cultivation of the mental fortitude to endure. Those who endure do not merely build companies; they build legacies that stand the test of time.

5.1 THE REALITIES OF STARTUP LIFE: GRIT AND PERSEVERANCE

Let us dispel the illusions that cloud the minds of those who gaze upon the glittering facade of startup success. In its naivety, the world fixates on unicorn valuations, fleeting billion-dollar exits, and headline-grabbing IPOs. But I tell you, these are mere shadows cast by the true substance of achievement. What they fail to perceive—the essence that defines enduring triumph—is the relentless battle waged behind the scenes. It is during the sleepless nights when product issues threaten to derail a crucial demonstration that a founder's mettle is tested. It's the desperate scramble to meet payroll when financial runway shrinks to a thread that reveals the true character. It is the moments of crushing self-doubt, when the very purpose of the endeavour is questioned, that forge spirit in the fires of adversity.

The media, ever eager to glorify the end result, conveniently ignores the arduous process, the brutal journey that breaks the vast majority. If you seek security, predictability or a balanced existence, then entrepreneurship is not your path. It is a war zone, a crucible where only the most resolute survive. To emerge victorious, you must possess more than talent; you must cultivate an unwavering grit.

What Is Grit? The Difference between Winners and Quitters

Angela Duckworth, a keen observer of human achievement, defines grit as 'passion and perseverance for long-term goals.' This seemingly simple definition encapsulates a rare and precious quality. Most people surrender by default when faced with the complexities and trials of the entrepreneurial journey. Talent, I assure you, is commonplace. Intelligence, likewise, is ordinary. Great ideas, those fleeting sparks of inspiration, are shared by many. But persistence, the unwavering ability to continue when all seems lost, is a rare and invaluable trait. Grit is the essence that separates the founders who endure from those who fade into obscurity.

Sridhar once had the opportunity to mentor a founder who was navigating a particularly turbulent phase of his entrepreneurial journey. He was facing a series of setbacks that shook his confidence and made him question his ability to succeed. Recognizing the crucial role that resilience plays in achieving long-term goals, Sridhar decided to introduce him to Angela Duckworth's grit framework. This framework, with its emphasis on passion and perseverance, provided a structured approach to cultivating the mental fortitude necessary to overcome challenges and achieve lasting success.

We began by setting clear, measurable objectives by breaking down his overarching vision into smaller, more manageable milestones. This not only gave him a sense of direction but also instilled a sense of accomplishment as he achieved each incremental goal. We also worked to cultivate a growth mindset, encouraging him to view challenges not as insurmountable obstacles but as opportunities for learning and development.

To further improve his resilience, we introduced the concept of deliberate practice, encouraging him to focus on targeted areas for improvement and to keep pushing beyond his comfort zone. This not only honed his skills but also instilled a sense of mastery and self-efficacy.

The transformation was remarkable. As he internalized the principles of the grit framework, his resilience grew, and he approached challenges with renewed vigour and determination. He learnt to see setbacks not as defeats but as valuable feedback, and he used them to refine his strategies and emerge stronger.

Ultimately, he not only overcame the challenges he faced but also achieved a level of success that once seemed unattainable. His story serves as a powerful testament to the transformative power of grit and the importance of cultivating a mindset that embraces challenges as opportunities for growth.

Why Grit Matters More than Intelligence, Ideas or Luck

Contrary to popular belief, it is not just intelligence that is rewarded in the startup world. If it did, our universities would be filled with billionaires. Nor does it solely reward ideas. If it did, the first person to envision a social network, not Mark Zuckerberg, would have built Facebook. And certainly, it does not solely reward luck. Many who experience initial success through serendipity falter in their subsequent ventures, having failed to cultivate resilience. It is grit, that unwavering determination, that makes all the decisive difference. It is the ability to press forward even when your product launch falters, your initial customers abandon you, and your investors withdraw their support, your co-founder quits, or the market shifts beneath your feet. Every legendary founder has faced these trials. The distinction lies in their unwavering commitment to perseverance.

The Slack Saga: From Gaming Flop to Communication Giant

Stewart Butterfield, a name now synonymous with seamless workplace communication, did not arrive at success on a gilded chariot. His initial venture, a massively popular multiplayer online game called Glitch, ultimately ran into the cold, unyielding wall of market disinterest despite years of fervent labour and significant investment. Many would have succumbed to the crushing weight of such a failure, retreating into the shadows of disillusionment. But Butterfield, who possessed that rare, indomitable spirit, refused to give up. He recognized within the discarded remnants of Glitch a powerful communication tool, a spark of potential that others had overlooked. He seized this ember, fanning it with relentless dedication, refining it and transforming it into what we know today as Slack. He endured the whispers of doubt, the sting of past failures, and the daunting task of pivoting an entire project. He faced the scepticism of investors and the indifference of a market that had already rejected his initial creation. But he pressed on, driven by an inner fire, by the conviction that his vision held true power. Would you, my friend, have the fortitude to extract a diamond from the ashes of a failed venture, to see opportunity where others see only ruin, to transmute the bitter taste of defeat into the sweet nectar of triumph? Most would not. And that, precisely, is why most will never build transformative, industry-defining enterprises.

How to Develop Grit As a Founder

Grit is not an innate trait, but a quality cultivated through deliberate effort. To succeed as a founder, you must train your resilience like a muscle, strengthening it through persistent exercise. View failure as a learning experience, not a personal defeat. The most successful founders view setbacks as valuable data, using them to adjust their course and try again. Fall in love with the problem you are solving, not just your original idea. Ideas can fail, but problems endure. If your first solution falters, pivot, but never lose sight of the core issue. Normalize rejection. Investors will decline, customers will ignore, and the media will remain indifferent. Persevere anyway.

Develop 'mental reserves' by deliberately placing yourself in uncomfortable situations. The more adversity you face, the stronger you become. Surround yourself with resilient individuals, for weak teams succumb to pressure. Hire those who have weathered storms and thrive in uncertainty. Cultivate long-term thinking, for expecting immediate success leads to premature surrender. Every successful startup requires years of dedication. Be prepared to outlast your competition.

The Reality: Most People Quit Too Soon

Success in the startup arena follows a simple but profound formula: Most founders abandon their ventures within the first year. Those who survive year one often succumb by year three. And those who endure past year three tend to dominate their respective markets. And why? Because grit compounds every time you overcome adversity, strengthening your resolve and giving you an edge over those who falter. Consider this: How many individuals possessed the potential to start Facebook but lacked perseverance? How many startups could have become Amazon but surrendered in year two? How many founders had ideas as revolutionary as Tesla but lacked the patience to execute them over decades? The startup world is not a sprint; it is an endurance test.

If You Quit, Nothing Else Matters

Grit is the defining factor that separates failure from success. You may possess the perfect idea, the most brilliant team, and ample funding, but if you abandon your endeavour when faced with adversity, you will inevitably fail. You will experience moments when the task seems insurmountable. You will question the value of your efforts. You will feel exhausted, rejected and tempted to surrender. Every great founder has faced these trials. The difference lies in their unwavering commitment to persevere. For in the end, it is not the smartest or the luckiest who prevail, but those who refuse to quit.

5.2 HOW TO HANDLE FAILURE AND REJECTION

Let me tell you, my friend, that failure is the tuition for the entrepreneurial school. Everyone who has ever forged a path of significance has tasted the bitter draught of rejection, been dismissed with a wave of the hand, and dropped out before the race had even begun—and often this occurs not just once but many times. The crucial distinction between those who etch their names in the annals of history and those who fade into the shadows of obscurity is simple: some allow failure to define who they are, while others seize it as the bedrock on which to rebuild themselves, stronger and more resilient than before. Rejection and failure are not mere obstacles to be skirted; they are the ultimate proving grounds for one's mettle. If you cannot stomach the sting of rejection, you are ill-prepared to navigate the tumultuous seas of building a venture.

Rejection Is Not a Dead End—It's a Data Point

An average individual takes rejection as a personal affront. A truly exceptional entrepreneur, on the other hand, sees rejection as invaluable market research. Are investors turning their backs on you? This is not a condemnation of your worth but a sign that your pitch lacks the compelling force it requires, or that you are courting the wrong audience. Customers show no interest in your product? This is a stark reminder that you have not yet unearthed a problem of sufficient magnitude, or that you have failed to articulate the value you offer with sufficient clarity. Are talented people declining your offers? This is a call to strengthen your company's vision and cultivate an alluring team culture. A rejection is not the final chapter; it is merely a data point, a piece of feedback. Every 'no' you receive is a clue, a guidepost pointing you toward the improvements that must be made.

> Shreeram recalls a promising startup that was struggling to secure funding. Their pitch, while technically sound, lacked one crucial element—a deep understanding of investor motivations. They presented their solution as a groundbreaking innovation but failed to connect it to the specific pain points that kept investors up at night.

> Recognizing this disconnect, Shreeram introduced them to the SPIN selling method.[30] SPIN selling is a consultative sales methodology that uses four types of questions (**s**ituation, **p**roblem, **i**mplication and **n**eed-payoff) to understand customer needs, build relationships and guide prospects towards recognizing the value of a solution.
>
> We meticulously analysed the current investment landscape, identifying the challenges, concerns and unmet needs of potential investors. We then reframed their pitch to directly address these pain points, demonstrating that the solution not only offered a technological edge but is also perfectly aligned with investor priorities.
>
> The transformation was remarkable. Their pitch was less about showcasing their innovation and more about demonstrating a deep understanding of the investor's perspective. This shift in approach resonated with investors and ultimately led to a successful funding round. It was a powerful reminder that even the most brilliant ideas need to be presented in a way that speaks directly to the needs and motivations of the audience.

Early Failures That Led to Multi-Billion-Dollar Companies

Take Kunal Shah before he built CRED. He founded FreeCharge, a mobile phone recharging and payments company, without any funding and without an established network in the venture capital world. In those early days, he faced relentless rejection, and the business teetered on the brink of collapse. Nevertheless, he did not surrender. He refined his pitch, iterated on his product, and transformed FreeCharge into one of India's fastest growing fintech startups, which eventually led to its acquisition by Snapdeal for $450 million. Years later, he harnessed the lessons learnt from FreeCharge—both the successes and the failures—to build CRED, a company that is now valued at over $6 billion. Remember, a failed pitch does not equal a failed business, and a failed business is not a sign of a failed entrepreneur.

The Right Kind of Failure vs the Wrong Kind of Failure

Not all failures are equal. There is a great chasm between failing intelligently and failing foolishly. Smart failure means launching quickly, testing assumptions, and iterating based on real customer feedback. Foolish failure, on the other hand, involves building a product in isolation for years, ignoring market signals, and refusing to adapt. Take Sridhar Vembu, the founder of Zoho. He built his company without external funding, focused on a global SaaS market before most Indian startups even thought of it, and took numerous strategic risks. Some of these risks did not bear fruit, but from each one he learnt invaluable lessons that allowed him to refine Zoho's business model.

Today, Zoho is a $10+ billion global company. Had Sridhar allowed the fear of failure to paralyse him, Zoho would never have come to fruition.

How to Handle Investor Rejection (without Letting It Kill Your Business)

Many startups falter in their quest for funding, not because their ideas are inherently flawed, but because their founders approach the process in a flawed manner.

Why Investors Say No (And What It Means)

Investors may tell you, 'The market is too small,' which means you have not demonstrated the potential for scalability. Or they might say, 'Your traction isn't enough,' which means you need stronger proof points. Or 'We're not interested right now,' which signifies they doubt your ability to execute. Deepinder Goyal, the founder of Zomato, faced countless rejections, cold-emailing VCs only to be ignored or turned away. But he persisted, refining his pitch until he secured the capital he needed to scale. Zomato transformed from a small food review website to a multi-billion-dollar IPO. The lesson is clear: an investor rejection is rarely a judgement on your idea per se; it reflects how effectively you communicate your opportunity.

When to Accept Failure vs When to Push Forward

There is a delicate balance between unwavering determination and blind stubbornness. A good pivot involves recognizing when the market doesn't want what you are building and shifting to what it does want. Bad stubbornness, on the other hand, means investing time and resources in an idea that the market has already rejected.

How Freshworks Pivoted to Win

When Girish Mathrubootham founded Freshworks, his vision was to develop a helpdesk tool for small businesses in India. However, the market proved too limited. Instead of clinging to a flawed model, he pivoted Freshworks to target a global audience, competing directly with giants like Zendesk and Salesforce. This pivot propelled Freshworks from a struggling niche player to India's first SaaS company to go public on the Nasdaq. The difference between success and failure often lies in knowing when to pivot.

> Sridhar recalls a founder he once mentored who was paralysed by the fear of failure. Every decision he made, every step he took, was laden with the anxiety of potential setbacks. He was so focused on avoiding mistakes that he was stifling his own progress.
>
> To help him overcome this debilitating fear, Sridhar introduced him to the build-measure-learn loop,[31] a core principle of the lean startup method.
>
> The build-measure-learn loop is a core principle of the lean startup method that emphasises an iterative process where startups build an MVP, measure its performance through customer feedback, and learn from the results to refine or pivot their product offering.
>
> Sridhar explained how by rapidly launching an MVP and iterating based on real user feedback, he could transform failure from a dreaded outcome into a valuable learning opportunity.
>
> The shift in his mindset was remarkable. He embraced the idea of experimentation, viewing each setback not as a defeat but as a stepping stone to a better product. He began to actively seek user feedback, using it to refine his offering and tailor it to the needs of the market.
>
> Through this iterative process, he not only overcame his fear of failure but also developed a product that truly resonated with his target audience. He learnt that failure, when seen as a learning tool, can be the catalyst for extraordinary success.

Turning Failure into Competitive Advantage

Failure is not the antithesis of success; it is a prerequisite for it. The most resilient founders turn failure into momentum. They meticulously document their mistakes to avoid repeating them; they view failure as a learning experience rather than a defeat; and they view obstacles as a filter, believing that if their startup can survive them, it deserves to exist. Take Ravi Kumar, the founder of GIVA, a jewellery brand that sells silver, gold and lab-grown diamond jewellery. His first jewellery startup failed because he misjudged demand and pricing. But he did not surrender. Instead, he applied the lessons learnt to launch GIVA with superior positioning. Today, GIVA is a market leader in online jewellery sales. Had he allowed his first failure to define him, GIVA would never have existed.

Mental Resilience: Handling Public Failure without Losing Confidence

The most formidable challenge of failure is not the loss itself but the way it is perceived by others. Investors remember your failed ventures, friends and family may question your choices, and the media, if they take notice, may label it a disaster.

The most successful founders don't allow noise to dictate their confidence. Take Shashank N.D., the founder of Practo, a digital health platform that connects patients with doctors, clinics, hospitals and other healthcare professionals. He faced numerous early setbacks, including investor rejections, slow market adoption and operational challenges. But he used these failures to refine Practo's model. Today, Practo is a multi-million-dollar healthcare platform that has outlasted many of its competitors. Had he taken the rejection personally, he would have abandoned Practo before it could reach its potential.

The Market Doesn't Punish Failure, It Punishes Stagnation

The world cares little about your failures; it cares deeply about your refusal to learn and adapt. Failure becomes a stepping stone, not a roadblock, when you continuously learn, adapt and improve. Most individuals never dare to take risks because they fear failure, and most founders give up after their first rejection. But those who analyse their failures, extract value from rejection, and iterate faster than their competitors are the ones who build companies that reshape the world.

5.3 KNOWING WHEN TO PIVOT (AND WHEN TO HOLD STEADY)

The greatest test of a founder's mettle is not the mere conception of an idea but the discerning wisdom to recognize whether that idea is destined to thrive. Some, in their haste, abandon a promising venture at the first sign of hardship, succumbing to the trials of early development. Others cling to a failing concept with stubborn persistence, squandering precious resources. The true challenge, my friends, is not simply how to build something but how to distinguish between flawed execution and a fundamentally flawed idea. The ability to know when to pivot and when to persevere is the very essence that separates the startup that scales from the one that collapses.

What Is Pivot?

Let's be clear: A pivot is not a whim, not just a change of heart. It is a deliberate, strategic shift, born from keen observation and market feedback. A soft pivot, a mere adjustment of a feature, business model or pricing strategy, refines your course within the same market. A hard pivot, however, demands a radical change, a complete redirection, perhaps even a venture into an entirely new industry.

This is not a reaction to frustration but a calculated move based on the irrefutable language of data. The most astute founders do not pivot out of weariness but because the numbers, those silent sentinels of truth, have spoken.

> Shreeram consulted a founder who was floundering, desperately seeking its footing in a saturated market. They had poured their hearts and souls into developing a truly innovative product, but despite their best efforts, they were struggling to gain traction. It was as if they were sailing in a stormy sea, their ship tossed about by the relentless waves of competition with no clear direction in sight.
>
> Observing their predicament, Shreeram recognized the need for a strategic intervention, a shift of perspective that would allow them to navigate these treacherous waters and chart a course for success. He introduced them to the blue ocean strategy,[32] a framework that emphasises the creation of uncontested market space rather than competing head-on with rivals.
>
> Blue ocean strategy is a business approach that focuses on creating new, uncontested market space through differentiation and low cost, making the competition irrelevant and unlocking new demand.

> Together, we embarked on a journey of discovery, meticulously analysing the competitive landscape and identifying untapped opportunities. We dissected their existing value proposition, questioned long-held assumptions, and challenged them to think beyond the confines of their current market.
>
> Through this process, a remarkable transformation began to unfold. The team's initial frustration gradually gave way to a sense of excitement as they realized the enormous potential that lay before them. They began to see their product not just as a solution to an existing problem but as a catalyst for creating an entirely new market, one where they could reign supreme. With renewed clarity and purpose, they redefined their value proposition by tailoring it to the unique needs of a previously overlooked customer segment. They shifted their focus from competing on features and price to creating an unparalleled customer experience that resonated deeply with their target audience.
>
> The results were nothing short of remarkable. The company's growth trajectory, once stagnant, suddenly surged. They had discovered their blue ocean, a vast expanse of uncontested market space where they could thrive and prosper. Their success was a testament to the power of strategic thinking, the importance of market validation, and the transformative potential of the blue ocean strategy.

When to Pivot: The Three Red Flags

Not every obstacle demands a pivot. Some challenges are merely a test of your execution. However, there are three unmistakable signals that demand a fundamental reassessment. First, no market demand is the deadliest sign of all. If your product fails to stir the hearts of customers despite tireless efforts, you are attempting to solve a problem that exists only in your mind. Remember that startups do not perish due to lack of funds but from a lack of purpose. Remember the story of Brandon Krieg, who sought to illuminate the masses with financial literacy, only to discover that they craved tools, not education. His pivot, the creation of Stash, stands as a testament to the power of listening to the market. If customers consistently ignore your offerings, you possess not a business but a mere hobby. Pivot, I say!

Second, the negative unit economics is a treacherous pitfall. Many a founder has been seduced by the illusion of volume, believing that higher sales would magically erase losses. But no amount of scaling can rectify a fundamentally broken model. The story of Housing.com, a once-promising real estate venture, is a stark reminder. Despite vast resources and a visionary team, their costs consistently outweighed their earnings. The refusal to pivot led to the company's demise. When the cost of acquiring customers exceeds their lifetime value, you are not building a startup but a financial abyss. Pivot or face the inevitable.

Third, major market shifts can render even the most robust businesses obsolete. Technological disruption, regulatory changes and shifting consumer behaviour can alter the landscape overnight. Take MakeMyTrip, whose existence was threatened by the COVID-19 pandemic. The company's survival hinged on their ability to adapt and pivot to domestic travel and new revenue streams. When the rules of the game change, your survival depends on your agility.

Sridhar recalls a particular startup that sought his counsel, their path fraught with peril as they navigated the treacherous waters of entrepreneurship. They were, in essence, a living embodiment of the three red flags Sridhar had outlined: a founder deeply enamoured with his own idea, a team hesitant to engage with potential customers, and a product languishing in development for far too long without any tangible evidence of market demand.

Recognizing the urgency of their situation, Sridhar guided them towards the principles of the lean startup method, emphasising the iterative build-measure-learn cycle as a means of rapidly testing their assumptions and discovering a viable market fit.

We encouraged them to shed their reluctance and engage in direct conversations with potential customers, gather invaluable feedback, and confront the uncomfortable reality that their initial vision might not align with the needs of the market.

This data-driven pivot proved to be their salvation. Armed with a newfound understanding of their target audience, they were able to recalibrate their product strategy, realign their development efforts, and ultimately achieve a success level that previously seemed unattainable. Their story serves as a potent reminder that the entrepreneurial journey is not a linear path but rather a series of experiments, iterations and course corrections guided by the unwavering pursuit of customer validation.

When to Hold Steady: Three Signals That Mean You Should NOT Pivot

Not every struggle demands a pivot. Sometimes persistence is the path to victory. First, short-term struggles are not market failures. If your challenges are rooted in execution, address them. If customers adore your product but delivery falters, refine your operations. If revenue is sluggish, tweak your sales process. Unacademy's early struggles to persevere through monetization challenges are a testament to the power of optimization. If your fundamentals are strong, optimize; do not pivot.

Second, temporary market fluctuations are not permanent. Do not be swayed by the ebb and flow of the market. The rise of Polygon, which remained steadfast during crypto downturns, demonstrates the wisdom of patience. Know the difference between a fleeting storm and a collapsing trend.

Third, if your core idea is strong, growth can be slow—but it's worth it. Don't confuse slow growth with failure. Many world-changing companies, such as Freshworks and Grammarly, took years to find their footing. The right idea, executed with diligence, will eventually find its moment.

The Pivot Decision: A Simple Framework

When faced with the dilemma of whether to pivot or persist, ask yourself: Is the problem rooted in execution or in the market? Are customers engaged but not converting, or are they completely disinterested? Are external forces rendering your model obsolete, or are you merely facing the trials of startup life? A premature pivot can kill momentum, while a delayed pivot can deplete your resources. But the right pivot at the right moment can birth a legend.

The Best Founders Are Adaptable, Not Reckless

Pivoting is not a sign of defeat but a strategic manoeuvre. The stories of Slack, Shopify and Instagram are proof of this. But the wisest founders pivot not just because the path is arduous but because the market demands it. Listen, adapt and execute. Pivot too soon, and you stifle a promising idea. Pivot too late, and you squander your resources. Pivot at the right moment, and you will build something unstoppable.

5.4 AVOIDING FOUNDER BURNOUT AND BUILDING MENTAL TOUGHNESS

Burnout Is the Silent Startup Killer

Let's be clear: Most ventures don't crumble due to a flawed concept or a lack of market. No, the true culprit is far more insidious—founder burnout. These founders labour under a delusion, believing that relentless toil-until-collapse is the measure of their dedication. They convince themselves that any less than an 18-hour grind is a sign of weakness. This, I tell you, is a poison to the mind, a self-inflicted wound. A startup is not a sprint; it's an ultramarathon. To push oneself beyond the breaking point is to render oneself useless when the company demands your utmost. The truly exceptional founders, those who leave their mark upon the world, are not those who sacrifice all but those who construct systems that allow them to endure for years. Without the mastery of mental resilience, recovery and balance, failure is assured.

The Truth About Founder Burnout

Burnout is not merely exhaustion; it is the transformation of exhaustion into apathy. Exhaustion is a state from which one can recover through rest, sleep and rejuvenation. Burnout, however, is the extinguishing of passion. You wake up, and the fire that once fuelled you has gone out. Resentment festers towards the very enterprise you birthed. This, my friends, is perilous. A startup demands a founder fully engaged—heart and soul. To reach a point of apathy is to seal the business's doom. And the most treacherous aspect? Burnout sneaks up on you, like a silent thief, while you delude yourself with the mantra 'just a little more push'. Then one day you find yourself shattered.

> Shreeram once mentored a founder who was on the brink of burnout. The weight of countless responsibilities, the relentless pressure to succeed, and the ever-present fear of failure had taken a toll on his well-being. He was drowning in a sea of urgent tasks, his energy depleted, his focus fragmented.
>
> Recognizing the urgency of the situation, Shreeram introduced him to the Eisenhower Matrix,[33] a powerful tool for prioritizing tasks based on their urgency and importance.
>
> The Eisenhower Matrix is a time management tool that categorizes tasks into four quadrants based on urgency and importance to help prioritize actions: do, schedule, delegate, or eliminate.
>
> Together, we meticulously categorized his responsibilities, distinguishing between those that truly demanded his immediate attention and those that could be delegated or deferred.

> The results were transformative. By offloading non-essential tasks and streamlining his workflow, he was able to reclaim his focus and direct his energy towards the strategic priorities that truly mattered. The sense of overwhelm dissipated, replaced by a renewed sense of clarity and purpose.
>
> This shift not only alleviated his stress but also significantly improved his efficiency. He became more decisive, more strategic, and more effective in his leadership. His company, once burdened by his dwindling energy, began to thrive under his revitalized guidance.
>
> This experience reinforced a fundamental truth: A founder's well-being is not a luxury, it is a necessity. By prioritizing self-care and implementing effective strategies for managing stress and overwhelm, founders can not only safeguard their own health and happiness but also unlock their full potential as leaders, driving their companies to new heights of success.

Why Founders Burn out

Many err in believing that burnout is merely the result of excessive labour. While that plays a part, the true root lies in mental mismanagement.

1. **Founders work 18-hour days without a system for recovery:** Too many founders treat sleep, exercise and health as optional luxuries. They forsake workouts for 'pressing matters', convince themselves that four hours of sleep suffice, and subsist on caffeine, junk food and stress. The body, however, will not be denied. It begins

with subtle signs—frequent illness, diminished focus and waning energy—before culminating in a complete collapse.
2. **Founders internalize every setback as a personal failure:** Rejection, failure and setback are seen as proof of inadequacy. An investor's refusal becomes a personal indictment, an employee's departure a sign of poor leadership, and slow growth a declaration of unsuitability. This self-destructive narrative breeds crippling stress. When one's self-worth is tethered to the startup's success, burnout is inevitable.
3. **Founders neglect health, relationships and sanity for the business:** Founders often sacrifice everything—relationships, social life, even self-care. Family events are cancelled, exercise is abandoned, and isolation is embraced, all in the name of dedication. Yet, loneliness, poor health and isolation lead to mental breakdown. A founder who succumbs to burnout is not a hero but a liability.

How to Build Mental Toughness and Avoid Burnout

1. **Detach from outcomes—your startup is not you:** The wisest founders maintain psychological distance from their ventures. A company's struggles do not equate to personal failure. A product flop is a mere data point, not a judgement on your intelligence. An investor's rejection does not diminish your worth.
2. **Systematize recovery—treat rest like an investment:** Those who endure treat recovery as a vital part of their work. Exercise daily, for it sharpens the mind. Prioritize sleep, for the brain thrives on rest. Practise mindfulness or meditation to manage stress. Take one day off weekly, for inspiration often arrives when you step away. Plan for longevity, not just fleeting bursts of activity.

3. **Find founder allies—entrepreneurship is lonely but it doesn't have to be:** To tread this path alone is a grave mistake. Seek out founder peer groups, surround yourself with seasoned mentors, and maintain open communication with co-founders. Remember Naval Ravikant's wisdom: 'Play long-term games with long-term people' and 'find allies who lift you up, not drag you down.' Survival is far easier when you have companions on the journey.

Burnout Is Optional: Resilience Is a Choice

The startup world, in its folly, glorifies suffering. Eighteen-hour days are not a badge of honour, and the neglect of health, sleep and relationships is not dedication but destruction. A fallen founder builds nothing. You are your startup's most valuable asset. If you burn out, the company burns with you. The greatest founders do not merely hustle; they endure. They do not merely sacrifice; they sustain. They do not merely survive; they thrive. Longevity, I tell you, is true victory. Cultivate resilience, or your startup will outlive you.

5.5 LEARNING FAST AND STAYING AHEAD OF MARKET TRENDS

The Only Sustainable Advantage Is Speed of Learning

Let it be known, my friends, that in the relentless pursuit of lasting success, the sole unwavering advantage is the swiftness of your learning. Startups, those engines of progress, are not mere vessels for idle ideas; they are forged in the crucible of execution, driven by the relentless pace of knowledge acquisition. If you aspire to erect a monument that withstands the sands of time, you must become an insatiable seeker of knowledge, a master of pattern recognition, and a virtuoso of real-time adaptation. The market, that capricious beast, will not tarry for your convenience. Consumer behaviour, like shifting wind, can alter overnight. Technology, that relentless force, advances at a pace that leaves regulations trailing in its wake. What served you yesterday may be utterly obsolete tomorrow. The founders who ascend to the heights of achievement are learning machines, pure and simple. They do not rely on the fickle hand of luck or the dubious guidance of gut instinct. They absorb data, trends, insights, and even the bitter lessons of failure with unwavering determination, and they apply this hard-won knowledge before their competitors even grasp its significance. A slow learner in the startup arena is a founder destined for oblivion.

Sridhar recalls a particularly challenging engagement with a burgeoning startup grappling with the complexities of adaptation in a rapidly evolving market. They were, as many young companies are, laser-focused on the immediate demands of their core business, tirelessly striving to optimize operations and maximize efficiency. However, in their relentless pursuit of short-term gains, they had inadvertently neglected the critical imperative of long-term innovation.

Recognizing this precarious imbalance, Sridhar introduced them to McKinsey's Three Horizons Model[34], a framework that elegantly delineates the different horizons of growth and innovation. The first horizon represents the core business, where the focus is on maximizing the value of existing products and services. The second horizon encompasses emerging opportunities and extensions of the core business, while the third horizon is dedicated to exploring disruptive innovations and future bets that could redefine the company and its industry.

By embracing this model, the startup was able to effectively categorize and structure its efforts across these three horizons. They allocated resources to optimize their core business, ensuring its continued profitability and stability, while simultaneously empowering teams to explore emerging opportunities and experiment with potentially disruptive innovations. This strategic realignment fostered a culture of continuous learning and experimentation, enabling the company to adapt to market shifts, anticipate future trends, and ultimately gain a decisive competitive edge.

The Three Horizons Model proved to be a transformative framework, guiding the startup on a path of sustainable growth and innovation. It served as a constant reminder that while operational efficiency is essential for short-term success, a relentless focus on the future is what ultimately separates enduring companies from those that fade into obscurity.

The Two Types of Learning: Deep versus Fast

Understand, however, that not all learning is created equal. A true leader must master two distinct forms of knowledge acquisition. First, there is deep learning, the mastery of foundational knowledge within your industry and beyond. This is the bedrock upon which your understanding is built. Second, there is fast learning, the ability to absorb real-time market signals and react with alacrity before your competitors seize the opportunity. Most individuals err by focusing on one to the exclusion of the other. If you confine yourself to deep learning, you risk becoming an expert in a world that no longer exists. If you chase only the fleeting trends of fast learning, you will find yourself adrift without a strategic compass. The most formidable founders, however, master both.

Read voraciously; founders who don't read will lose

What, you may ask, distinguishes the average founder from those who reshape the very fabric of our world? The answer lies in the books they consume. Every founder of consequence is an obsessive learner. They do not limit themselves to the confines of business manuals; they devour knowledge across a multitude of disciplines. History teaches us how industries rise and fall, psychology illuminates the intricate workings of customer decision-making, and science and artificial intelligence reveal the shape of the future being constructed before our very eyes. The finest founders read fifty or more books each year, not merely to gather information but because they understand that insights, like compound interest, accumulate over time.

Talk to experts: Learning through proximity

Yet, the swiftest path to knowledge does not lie solely within the pages of books; it lies in proximity to those who already possess it. The astute founder does not squander precious time reinventing the wheel. Instead, they seek out experts, surround themselves with individuals of superior intellect, and absorb knowledge directly. Find mentors who have already built the very thing you aspire to create. Join founder groups where candid conversations flow freely. Attend niche industry events, not merely the grand, impersonal conferences.

Experiment aggressively: The market is the ultimate teacher

No book, no mentor, no expert, however wise, can substitute for the feedback gleaned from the real world. If you are not actively testing, failing, learning, and iterating, you are merely engaging in guesswork. Launch swiftly; if a year passes before your first product sees the light of day, you have already lost. Seek customer feedback without delay; every conversation is a lesson waiting to be learnt. Refine in real time; data trumps opinions every time. If something is not working, rectify it with haste.

> In our years guiding entrepreneurs through the intricate dance of building a business, Shreeram encountered individuals with remarkable expertise in their respective fields, yet often lacking the agility to navigate the ever-shifting tides of the marketplace. One such founder, a brilliant mind steeped in the depths of deep learning, found himself struggling to adapt to the rapid pace of the startup world. He possessed an unparalleled understanding of complex algorithms and neural networks, but the dynamic nature of customer needs and market trends seemed to elude his grasp.
>
> Recognizing his immense potential yet acknowledging his need for a framework to accelerate his learning and decision-making, we introduced him to the OODA loop,[35] a concept developed by Colonel John Boyd, a renowned fighter pilot and military strategist. The OODA loop, which stands for **o**bserve, **o**rient, **d**ecide, **a**ct, emphasises the importance of rapid, iterative cycles of learning and action in dynamic environments.

> Shreeram explained to him how this principle, born out of the crucible of aerial combat, could be applied with equal effectiveness to the challenges of building and scaling a startup. We worked together to cultivate his ability to systematically observe market signals, orient himself within the competitive landscape, make swift decisions based on the information at hand, and act decisively to capitalize on opportunities or mitigate risks.
>
> The transformation was remarkable. As he internalized the principles of the OODA loop, his agility increased exponentially. He became more attuned to the nuances of customer feedback, more adept at deciphering market trends, and more decisive in his actions. The result was a marked improvement in the trajectory of his startup, as he consistently made better decisions, reacted more quickly to emerging challenges, and ultimately achieved greater success.
>
> This experience reinforced my belief that while deep expertise is undoubtedly valuable, it is the ability to learn and adapt quickly that truly sets apart the most successful entrepreneurs. The OODA loop, with its emphasis on rapid iteration and decisive action, serves as a powerful tool for navigating the complexities of the startup world and achieving extraordinary outcomes.

Why Most Founders Fail to Learn at Startup Speed

Most founders do not fail due to a lack of intelligence; they fail because they lack the agility to learn rapidly enough. They cling to past knowledge, oblivious to its obsolescence. They await perfect answers while the market races ahead. They fear being proven wrong, when in truth the greatest lessons are born of testing, not theorizing.

The 'Kodak Moment' of Startups

Consider the cautionary tale of Kodak, which invented the digital camera in 1975 yet failed to recognize its potential to supplant film. They ignored the signals of the market, underestimated the speed of adoption, and clung to outdated knowledge as the world transformed around them.

By the time they awoke to their folly, they were rendered obsolete. This fate befalls startups with alarming regularity. If you cling to outdated notions, you are already irrelevant.

How to Stay Ahead of Market Trends

If you wish to remain ahead of the curve, rather than being crushed beneath it, adhere to this formula. First, position yourself where the future is being built. Innovative founders discern trends before they become manifest. Scrutinize patent filings and research papers before they reach mainstream adoption. Follow high-signal thinkers, those researchers, venture capitalists and domain experts who shape the landscape, not the ephemeral influencers. Observe where the brightest minds are gravitating. The rise of decentralized AI startups, such as Together AI, MosaicML and Stability AI, exemplifies this principle. Together AI is a cloud-based platform that helps users train, fine-tune and deploy open-source AI models. MosaicML, recently acquired by Databricks, is a company specializing in developing technology that allows users to efficiently train large AI models, particularly large language models, on their own data, providing a platform to build and customize generative AI models at scale with a focus on cost-effectiveness and accessibility. Stability AI is a UK-based artificial intelligence company that develops generative AI models.

They foresaw the trend years before its mainstream recognition, building for a future problem before it was apparent. If you wait until a trend is mainstream, you are already too late. Second, cultivate the ability to think in first principles. Most follow conventional wisdom, but the greatest founders dissect problems into their fundamental truths. Ask 'why' five times, delving to the root cause. Question assumptions, for tradition is not synonymous with correctness. Rebuild from scratch, envisioning how you would construct your enterprise with today's technology and knowledge.

Learning Is the Only Competitive Advantage

In the final analysis, you will falter if you do not relentlessly consume knowledge, test ideas, and adapt to the feedback of the real world. Read more than your competitors, surround yourself with experts, and test ideas swiftly, embracing failure as a stepping stone to learning. The finest founders do not merely learn quickly; they outlearn everyone else. This is the path to staying ahead. This is the path to victory.

5.6 THE ENDURING IMPACT OF ENTREPRENEURSHIP

Why Do You Build?

Most individuals who embark upon the creation of a business do so for fleeting, superficial reasons. They are lured by the siren song of a temporary funding surge, the allure of a currently fashionable industry, or the deceptive promise of swift financial gain. They fixate upon exits, valuations, and the ephemeral glory of an initial public offering. However, the true architects of lasting enterprises, those who redefine industries and weather the relentless storms of market fluctuations, are driven by a far deeper, more profound purpose. They are the individuals who, upon witnessing the flaws and inadequacies of existing systems, refuse to passively accept them. They are consumed by an insatiable desire to bring into existence that which has never before been seen. They are driven by an unwavering obsession to craft something that transcends their own mortal existence. And herein lies the great paradox: those who chase solely the ephemeral chimera of monetary reward rarely attain it. Conversely, those who dedicate themselves to the resolution of significant problems are the ones who construct the iconic companies that generate wealth for generations. If your endeavour is solely motivated by the pursuit of financial gain, you will inevitably succumb to the crushing weight of burnout. But if you are building for a purpose greater than yourself, you will endure.

Entrepreneurship Is Industry-Altering, Not Just Profitable

The most impactful entrepreneurs do not merely accumulate wealth; they reshape the very fabric of our world. They redefine the operational paradigms of entire industries, they transform the way people live, and they shape the contours of the future. Consider, for example, companies such as Ripple, which did not simply create a fintech enterprise but challenged the very foundations of global financial settlements and revolutionized cross-border transactions. Or, consider Pixxel in India, which is not merely selling satellite images but also revolutionizing space technology by launching high-resolution earth observation satellites to tackle climate change, agriculture inefficiencies, and disaster prediction. Or Ginkgo Bioworks in the USA, which is not just building a biotech company but also engineering biology at scale, transforming pharmaceuticals, food production and materials science—a company that uses cell programming to create solutions for a variety of industries. They work with clients to create custom microbes for things like food, pharmaceuticals and industrial chemicals.

These are not merely vendors of products; they are the architects of industrial transformation, fundamentally altering the realm of what is possible.

If You Want to Build a Legacy, Solve Hard Problems

Some businesses merely offer incremental improvements, while others redefine entire markets. What, then, is the most direct path to constructing something that will endure? It is to tackle problems that truly matter. Embrace transformational change over incremental adjustments. Most companies are content to produce slightly improved versions of existing products. The most exceptional companies, however, create something ten times better or something entirely novel. If your creation can be easily replicated by another, your vision is not sufficiently grand. If your creation would not be missed if it vanished tomorrow, you are not addressing a genuine problem. High-stakes problems create high-stakes companies. If you aspire to build something that outlasts the fleeting hype of the market, you must confront industry-wide pain points. Consider SpaceX, which stepped in to define the future of space travel when government agencies faltered. Or consider Niramai, a novel artificial intelligence-based medical device to detect breast cancer at a much earlier stage than traditional methods or self-examination because traditional methods were failing millions of women. The harder the problem, the greater the opportunity. If a challenge is deemed too complex, too risky, or too premature by others, that is your signal to seize it. The radical approach to logistics adopted by Rivigo, a technology-driven logistics company based in India, primarily known for its unique 'relay driving' model, where drivers only drive for short stretches and are able to return home daily, stands as a testament to this truth. Instead of merely tweaking existing models, they fundamentally restructured an entire industry, introducing relay trucking and slashing delivery times, thereby solving both driver fatigue and operational inefficiency. The lesson is clear: the most enduring companies do not merely optimize existing models, they design entirely new ones.

Endurance: The Founders Who Refused to Quit

Entrepreneurship is not a sprint; it is a marathon. It is not about who initiates the race but who perseveres to the finish line. The most successful entrepreneurs share a common trait: they endure long enough to achieve victory. Startup failures rarely stem from flawed ideas; they arise from founders who abandon the fight before the breakthrough arrives. Freshworks, India's first NASDAQ-listed SaaS company, is a shining example of this principle. Girish Mathrubootham spent years battling global giants, facing scepticism and funding winters, yet he relentlessly refined his product and strategy.

Now, Freshworks stands as a testament to the power of endurance. The companies that endure are not always the fastest to grow; they are the ones that continue to improve long after others have surrendered.

Great Founders Think in Decades, Not Funding Cycles

Many entrepreneurs are ensnared by the pursuit of short-term gains, launching for funding rather than product-market fit, optimizing for valuation rather than sustainable business models, and exiting prematurely. The founders who reshape industries, however, possess a different mindset. They think in decades, not funding rounds or exits. They build for the long haul. Patrick Collison of Stripe is constructing an internet-native financial infrastructure designed to endure for generations. Deepinder Goyal of Zomato understood that food delivery was not merely about app installations but about controlling India's food supply chain. Ather Energy in India did not simply build another electric vehicle; they constructed India's electric vehicle ecosystem from its very foundations. If you aspire to build something that will endure, you must shift your perspective from the immediate future to the distant horizon.

Legacy over Hype: What Do You Want to Be Remembered For?

Entrepreneurs often become so consumed by the pursuit of growth, funding and competition that they neglect to ask themselves a fundamental question: What am I building that will outlast me? If your startup were to cease operations tomorrow, would the world feel its absence? Are you constructing something that will remain relevant in ten, twenty, or fifty years? Would your passion endure even if no one were watching?

The most exceptional entrepreneurs are driven by a burning desire to solve problems that transcend their own existence. They do not falter when challenges arise, nor do they deviate from their mission in response to investor demands. They build with unwavering endurance, knowing that true impact requires time.

Are You a Founder or a Builder?

There is a profound distinction between founding a company and constructing something that endures. Founders chase funding; builders chase mastery. Founders focus on valuation; builders focus on value creation. Founders seek exits; builders seek impact. The survivors are not merely founders; they are builders. The question is not 'how rapidly can I grow', but rather, 'how long can I build'. The entrepreneurs who endure are not merely remembered for their companies; they are remembered for reshaping the world.

The Journey Is the Reward

Ah, you've journeyed this far, a testament in itself. You comprehend, then, the very bedrock upon which a startup is erected. You grasp that entrepreneurship is not a fleeting chase after ephemeral hype but a steadfast endeavour to solve tangible, real-world problems. You understand that a magnificent product, devoid of salesmanship, is but a beautiful, useless artefact. You know that funding is a tool, not the ultimate prize, and that your team, your loyal band, is your most formidable competitive advantage. But let me impart a truth, a secret whispered only to those who dare to listen: the greatest founders, the ones who truly etch their names into the annals of success, do not triumph merely because they possess the most brilliant ideas. They prevail because they possess an unyielding refusal to relinquish their dreams. All that has come before—the strategies, the tactics, the market positioning, the financial manoeuvring, the growth mechanics, and the art of leadership—these are but tools in the craftsman's kit. No playbook, however meticulously crafted, can fully prepare you for the herculean task of birthing something from nothing. The ultimate crucible, the final test that separates the wheat from the chaff, is endurance.

Endurance: The Longest Mile

Passion and patience, those invisible forces, are the very lifeblood that sustains the entrepreneur when the storms of adversity rage. They are the driving forces that propel you through the treacherous terrains of uncertainty, the crushing blows of failure, and the relentless onslaught of setbacks that would shatter the resolve of lesser souls. This final chapter, then, is a deep dive into the internal theatre of entrepreneurship, the mastering of your own psychology, the cultivation of unwavering resilience, and the ability to outlast those who succumb to the siren song of premature surrender. Passion and patience are not mere suggestions; they are non-negotiable prerequisites for those who aspire to build something of lasting significance.

Passion is the only sustainable fuel in the engine of entrepreneurship. Not funding, not talent, not even the elusive product-market fit. These are mere sparks, fleeting and ephemeral. Passion is the eternal flame that keeps the furnace burning when all else turns to ash. Consider the founders who have weathered the storms, who have endured long enough to claim their rightful place in the pantheon of success. They did not triumph because they were intellectually superior to their competitors, but because they cared more, they burnt with a fiercer, more relentless fire. They obsessed over their chosen problem for years, even decades, before the world awakened to its significance. They sacrificed the comforts of security and predictability, driven by an inner compulsion, an inability to envision themselves pursuing any other path. They persisted through failures, not out of obligation, but because they were driven by an unyielding refusal to allow their vision to perish. Why, you ask, does passion outweigh strategy? Because passion cannot be manufactured, cannot be faked. It is an intrinsic force, either present or absent. The greatest founders do not embark on their ventures with the sole intent of a quick exit or a bloated valuation. They are driven by an insatiable obsession with the problem they seek to solve.

Nitin Saluja and Chaayos—The Relentless Pursuit of the Perfect Cup

Nitin Saluja was possessed by a simple yet revolutionary idea— chai, the beloved Indian tea, should be as customizable as coffee. While multinational giants flooded the Indian market with overpriced coffee shops, he saw an opportunity, a void waiting to be filled. He dedicated months to perfecting a brewing technology that would allow customers to customize their chai in over 80,000 ways. He refused to compromise on quality, ensuring that every outlet maintained the authentic taste and freshness that he envisioned. Investors, blinded by conventional wisdom, were sceptical. Why build a chain for something people made at home? But Nitin was not merely building a tea brand; he was building a movement. Today, Chaayos stands as one of India's most successful beverage chains. Would he have survived if he had chased funding alone? Impossible. Would he have persevered if he had sought a quick flip? Not a chance. Passion, not strategy, was his guiding star.

Passion sets the wheels in motion, but patience prevents them from spinning off the axle. The greatest adversary of the entrepreneur is not competition, nor a lack of funding, nor even the vagaries of the market. It is impatience. Founders abandon their visions too hastily, pivot too frequently, and chase fleeting short-term gains at the expense of long-term value. The most iconic companies of our era were often dismissed as failures for years before they emerged as category-defining behemoths.

The Story of Growing in the Shadows: GitHub

Take GitHub, a side project that blossomed into the backbone of global software development. For its first four years, it operated without external funding. The founders, wise beyond their years, refused to raise capital prematurely, focusing instead on organic, sustainable growth. While competitors chased the fleeting allure of hype, GitHub quietly solidified its position as an indispensable tool for developers. By the time it sought external investment, it was already a dominant force. Years later, Microsoft acquired it for a staggering $7.5 billion. Would GitHub have achieved such heights if it had rushed the process? Never. Patience was their strategic advantage.

Endurance: The Final Test

Most individuals are willing to endure hardship for a few months. Some can tolerate struggle for a few years. But the founders who truly reshape industries are those who possess the fortitude to grind for a decade or more. The world's most successful entrepreneurs share a common trait: they endure longer than anyone else. Most people falter when the going gets tough, and most founders pivot when they should persevere. The victors are those who simply refuse to yield.

The Final Test: What Will You Build?

Now, the pivotal question: What will you build that warrants such unwavering endurance? If your startup vanished tomorrow, would anyone truly care? If the next five years were fraught with challenges, would you still be in the arena? If success demanded a decade of unwavering commitment, would you possess the patience to see it through? The world does not yearn for more startups, serial entrepreneurs, or those chasing funding rounds. It craves builders, individuals with the resilience to endure.

The Entrepreneur's Leap

This book, this guide, provides you with the blueprint for identifying promising ideas, securing funding, mastering sales, building a formidable team, and navigating the mental gauntlet of entrepreneurship. But no book can transform you into an entrepreneur. This transformation is an inner alchemy, a personal leap of faith. You stand at the precipice, armed with knowledge. The only step left to take is the leap. You will face uncharted territories, suffer setbacks, and be tested in ways you cannot yet fathom. The question echoing in the corridors of your soul is: Will you persevere when the path becomes arduous? Most will falter, most will surrender, and most will concoct excuses. But those who endure, those who refuse to be deterred, they are the ones who reshape the fabric of the world. What will you do?

Acknowledgements

We express our heartfelt gratitude to the incredible incubation centres and startup ecosystems, including T-Hub, Stanford Seed, IIT Delhi, IIT Kanpur, IIT Mandi, BITS Pilani Hyderabad, TiE Global and Korea Startup Centre, for providing hundreds of opportunities to collaborate with and mentor their vibrant startups. These experiences have profoundly enriched our entrepreneurial journey.

Our sincere thanks go to the governments of Telangana, Andhra Pradesh, Rajasthan, Uttar Pradesh, Maharashtra and Madhya Pradesh. Their openness to dialogue, thoughtful policymaking, and commitment to entrepreneurship have empowered us to engage deeply with key decision-makers, shaping a brighter future for startups.

We are indebted to the countless entrepreneurs who have shared their journeys with us, trusting our advice and growing alongside us. Equally, we extend our appreciation to the investors who believed in us, invested in us, and continue working hand in hand to nurture promising portfolio ventures.

Finally, our deepest appreciation and gratitude go to our families, whose unwavering support, patience and love have been our most significant source of strength and inspiration throughout this journey.

Endnotes

1. Russell, Stuart, and Peter Norving, *Artificial Intelligence: A Modern Approach*, Pearson, London, 2021.
2. Maurya, Ash, *Running Lean: Iterate from Plan A to a Plan That Works*, O'Reilly Media, USA, 2012.
3. Ries, Eric. *The Lean Startup: How Today's Entrepreneurs Use Continuous Innovation to Create Radically Successful Businesses*, Currency, USA, 2011.
4. Kotler, Philip, and Lane Kelle Keller, *Marketing Management*. Pearson Education, USA, 2021.
5. Ibid.
6. Moore, Geoffrey A., *Inside the Tornado: Strategies for Developing, Leveraging and Surviving Hypergrowth Markets*, HarperCollins, USA, 2005.
7. Parker, G. G., et al., *Platform Revolution: How Networked Markets Are Transforming the Economy—and How to Make Them Work for You*, W. W. Norton & Company, New York, 2016.
8. Gothelf, Jeff, and Josh Seiden, *Lean UX: Applying Lean Principles to Improve User Experience*, O'Reilly Media, USA, 2013.
9. Maurya, Ash, *Running Lean: Iterate from Plan A to a Plan That Works*, O'Reilly Media, USA, 2012.

10. Pyhrr, Peter A., *Zero-Base Budgeting: A Practical Management Tool for Evaluating Expenses*, Wiley, New Jersey, 1977.
11. Ries, Eric, *The Lean Startup: How Today's Entrepreneurs Use Continuous Innovation to Create Radically Successful Businesses*, Currency, USA, 2011.
12. Bly, Robert W., *The Copywriter's Handbook: A Step-By-Step Guide to Writing Copy That Sells*, Holt Paperbacks, USA, 2005.
13. Christensen, C.M., et al., *Competing Against Luck: The Story of Innovation and Customer Choice*, HarperCollins, New York, 2016.
14. Naik, Gajesh, and Kevon Cheung, *Find Joy in Building in Public*, Public Lab, 2021.
15. An, Mimi, 'Topic clusters: The next evolution of SEO', *HubSpot*, 6 September 2017, https://tinyurl.com/5zw3rjj2. Accessed on 3 April 2025.
16. Pulizzi, J., *Epic Content Marketing: How to Tell a Different Story, Break Through the Clutter, and Win More Customers by Marketing Less*, McGraw-Hill Education, USA, 2014.
17. Sinek, Simon, *Start With Why: How Great Leaders Inspire Everyone to Take Action*, Portfolio, USA, 2009.
18. Siroker, Dan, and Pete Koomen, *A/B Testing: The Most Powerful Way to Turn Clicks Into Customers*, Wiley, New Jersey, 2013.
19. Eyal, N., *Hooked: How to Build Habit-Forming Products*, Portfolio, USA, 2014.
20. Smart, Geoff, and Randy Street, *Who: The A Method for Hiring*, Ballantine Books, USA, 2008.
21. Beck, K., et al., *Manifesto for Agile Software Development*, Agile Alliance, USA, 2001.

22 Wong, J., 'What does it mean to "hire slow, fire fast"?' *LinkedIn*, 2023.
23 Deci, Edward L., and Richard M. Ryan, *Intrinsic Motivation and Self-Determination in Human Behavior*, Springer, 1985.
24 Thaler, R.H., and C.R. Sunstein, *Nudge: Improving Decisions About Health, Wealth and Happiness*, Yale University Press, New York, 2008.
25 Carlson, Nicholas, 'EXCLUSIVE: How Mark Zuckerberg booted his co-founder out of the company', *Business Insider*, 15 May 2012, https://tinyurl.com/4jws7mrh. Accessed on 3 April 2025.
26 Sen, Anirban, 'Flipkart, and the Ballad of the Bansals', *Livemint*, 27 December 2018, https://tinyurl.com/y9d7h9e7. Accessed on 3 April 2025.
27 Mishra, Digbijay, 'Sachin Bansal, Kunal Bahl involved in Twitter spat', *Times of India*, 26 March 2016, https://tinyurl.com/29af89n3. Accessed on 3 April 2025.
28 Fisher, Roger, et al., *Getting to Yes: Negotiating Agreement Without Giving In*, Houghton Mifflin, USA, 1981.
29 'Monday Blog', https://tinyurl.com/4s7jrp2a, Accessed on 3 April 2025.
30 Rackham, Neil, *SPIN Selling*, McGraw-Hill Education, USA, 1988.
31 Blank, Steve, and Bob Dorf, *The Startup Owner's Manual: The Step-by-Step Guide for Building a Great Company*, Wiley, USA, 2013.
32 Mauborgne, R., and W.C. Kim, *Blue Ocean Strategy: How to Create Uncontested Market Space and Make the Competition Irrelevant*, Harvard Business Review Press, USA, 2005.
33 'Eisenhower Matrix', *TechTarget*, https://tinyurl.com/8kbn7aev. Accessed on 3 April 2025.

34 Baghai, Mehrdad, et al., *The Alchemy of Growth: Practical Insights for Building the Enduring Enterprise*, Basic Books, 1999.
35 Boyd, Col. John R., *A Discourse on Winning and Losing*, Air University Press, Alabama, 1987.